60 Innovative Cognitive Strategies for the Bright, the Sensitive, and the Creative

In this book, Dr. Maisel employs the metaphor of "the room that is your mind" to provide 60 cognitive strategies that enable smart, sensitive, creative clients to engage in dynamic self-regulation for greater awareness, insight, and enhanced mental capabilities. Issues that are examined include repetitive and obsessional thinking, self-criticism and a lack of self-confidence, anxiety and depression, reliving traumatic memories, and overdramatizing and catastrophizing. This is the perfect book for cognitive-behavioral therapists to suggest to clients and will be of great interest to clients whose needs for imaginative and metaphorically rich strategies often go unmet.

Eric Maisel, PhD, is a retired family therapist, creativity coach, and internationally respected expert in the field of mental health reform. He is the author of more than 50 books and reaches a substantial audience with his personal list, Psychology Today blog, print column for *Professional Artist Magazine*, guest editorship for parent resources at Mad in America, and weekly appearance in the *Fine Art America* newsletter.

60 Innovative Cognitive Strategies for the Bright, the Sensitive, and the Creative

New Investigations Into the Home of the Mind

Eric Maisel

Routledge
Taylor & Francis Group

NEW YORK AND LONDON

First published 2018
by Routledge
711 Third Avenue, New York, NY 10017

and by Routledge
2 Park Square, Milton Park, Abingdon, Oxon, OX14 4RN

Routledge is an imprint of the Taylor & Francis Group, an informa business

Library of Congress Cataloging-in-Publication Data
Names: Maisel, Eric, 1947– author.
Title: 60 innovative cognitive strategies for the bright, the sensitive and the creative : new investigations into the home of the mind / Eric Maisel.
Other titles: Sixty innovative cognitive strategies for the bright, the sensitive and the creative
Description: New York, NY : Routledge, 2018. | Includes index.
Identifiers: LCCN 2017048621| ISBN 9781138567023 (hardcover : alk. paper) | ISBN 9781138567030 (pbk. : alk. paper) | ISBN 9781351203753 (e-book)
Subjects: LCSH: Creative ability. | Artists – Psychology. | Artists – Mental health | Cognitive therapy. | Psychotherapist and patient.
Classification: LCC BF408 .M231947 2018 | DDC 153-dc23
LC record available at https://lccn.loc.gov/2017048621

ISBN: 978-1-138-56702-3 (hbk)
ISBN: 978-1-138-56703-0 (pbk)
ISBN: 978-1-351-20375-3 (ebk)

Typeset in Sabon
by HWA Text and Data Management, London

Contents

Introduction

This book is intended for helpers, for their clients, for smart, sensitive, creative individuals in distress, and for anyone interested in learning more about dynamic self-regulation, healthy indwelling, and innovative cognitive strategies for better mental health. I hope that you'll find the sixty exercises in Parts II and III of this book useful and enjoyable and the Part I explanations of dynamic self-regulation and healthy indwelling clear and compelling. Please enjoy!

As to helpers, I have in mind helpers who either largely or flat-out reject the two current, dominant mental health paradigms. First, they reject the claims made by proponents of the primary dominant paradigm that distress is a pseudo-medical condition that can be diagnosed and treated like medical illnesses. They likewise reject the validity of the bibles of that group, the DSM and the ICD, and reject the primary tactic of that group, chemical intervening.

They also reject the claims of proponents of the second dominant paradigm, that there exist certain classes of experts—psychotherapists, psychiatrists, clinical psychologists, etc.—who know for a fact what is causing a given individual's distress and who know for a fact what to do to relieve that distress. This second group tends to employ the bibles of the first group, even if they themselves are psychologically-oriented, and their primary tactic is expert-talk based on so-called theory. The helpers I have in mind are skeptical about all this.

Instead, these helpers embrace a third paradigm, the paradigm of humane helping (which I've described in *Humane Helping* (2017)), a paradigm of modesty and honesty where helpers forthrightly acknowledge all that they don't know and try to be of help by collaborating with their clients. The question that this helper is obliged to answer, then, is "What actually helps?" Humane helpers conclude that many things help: the warmth and support of another human being; acquiring new skills and new habits; changing one's outlook and circumstances; and more. Among these many is positive cognitive change.

A client can be helped a great deal if he learns to think thoughts that serve him better than his current thoughts do. He can be helped even more if he's taught to engage in what I am calling dynamic self-regulation, where he not only thinks thoughts that serve him but also enters into smart conversation with himself "in the room that is his mind." In that room, he indwells in ways that are fair to call unhealthier (say, in a claustrophobic, self-pestering way) or healthier (say, in an airy, calm, self-friendly way). Two sensible goals for humane helpers, whether or not they practice cognitive-behavioral therapy, are to promote dynamic self-regulation and healthy in-dwelling.

I also have a specific client in mind, though any client can benefit from these ideas and exercises. I've been working with smart, sensitive, creative clients for more than thirty years, first as a psychotherapist and then as a creativity coach. I know them and their issues and challenges well. I also know that they find the ideas of dynamic self-regulation and healthy indwelling congenial, even if hard to master, and enjoy the innovative cognitive strategies I'm providing in this book. If these clients are among your clientele, then this book is for you—and for them.

In Part I, I explain dynamic self-regulation and healthy indwelling and paint a picture of the challenges confronting smart, sensitive, creative individuals. In Part II, I present thirty cognitive strategies for improved mental health that any client might find useful. In Part III, I describe thirty cognitive strategies specially aimed at meeting the challenges facing smart, sensitive, creative clients. I hope that you and your clients find these ideas and exercises useful.

Part I
Dynamic Self-Regulation and Healthy Indwelling

1   Humane Help for Smart, Sensitive, Creative Clients

Smart, sensitive, creative clients—the folks most likely to engage in individual psychotherapy and individual coaching, given their psychological-mindedness, verbal skills, and basic orientation toward ideas like healing and growth—are both different from and not different from other human beings. To my mind, they are rather more different than not different. In a subsequent chapter, I'll explain in what ways they are different and how those differences present a humane helper with special challenges. In this chapter, I want to provide a bit of an overview and explain what I'm attempting to do in this book.

I've been working, first as a therapist and for thirty years as a creativity coach, with creative and performing artists, scientists and engineers, academics and entrepreneurs, and other bright, imaginative clients. All have been troubled in one way or another and most have ended up with some "mental disorder" label, maybe a depression, bipolar, attention deficit or generalized anxiety label—or with multiple mental disorder labels. Nor, to my mind, is this small sample non-representative of the whole. I believe that all smart, sensitive, creative people are troubled enough to earn some mental disorder label, if one believed in those labels, because there is a necessary connection between intelligence, sensitivity, creativity, and distress.

Being smart, sensitive, creative, *and* troubled go hand-in-hand. But the current system that calls these particular troubles "mental disorders" and rushes to prescribe chemicals is misguided. I've laid out the ways in which the current, dominant pseudo-medical paradigm is flawed in books like *The Future of Mental Health*, *Humane Helping*, *The Van Gogh Blues*, and *Rethinking Depression*. In this book, I want to present you with a robust way of helping these folks, a way that doesn't rely on the pseudo-medical "mental disorder" paradigm or on the second current dominant paradigm, the "expert talk" paradigm, either. Instead, I want to present a collaborative model that makes beneficial use of the cognitive and creative abilities that your smart, sensitive, creative clients possess.

These clients are bringing something more to the table in addition to their troubles. They are bringing an existential sensibility. They are bringing an imagination that can create worlds. They are bringing a love of language and metaphor. They are bringing an ability to get from the beginning of a thought to its end. They are bringing a taste for value. They are bringing respect for effort. They are bringing at least the remnants of a child's wonder. They are bringing laughter, however muffled, and love, however cooled. They may not be bringing quite everything they need to bring, but they are bringing a lot.

Say that a smart, sensitive, creative person comes in to see you complaining of "depression." All of the following may be true for him. He may have been born already a little sad. Reality may be making him sad. The hardness of his creative work may be making him sad. The harshness of the art marketplace may sadden him. The boring routine of his safe, "pointless" academic day job may be saddening him. So may the inevitable conflicts between wanting solitude and wanting relationships, preferring personal work to the commercial work that an audience wants, and so on.

On top of all that, he may have decided that life is a cheat, which saddens him even more. In addition, every bit of tyranny and injustice he encounters or hears about saddens him. His own shortfalls, for instance how often he dodges his creative work, saddens him. The criticism and rejection that his creative work regularly receives saddens him. This list is very long and could be much longer. What it causes is not a pseudo-medical mental disorder. It is sadness multiplied over and over again, culminating in despair. What human being *wouldn't* be deeply troubled by all this?

Might there also be some biological, neurological, hormonal, or similar reason for his unhappiness? Who can say? But isn't the above list quite enough to account for his despair? Why add other reasons for which there is zero proof? It is impossible to prove the non-existence of non-existing things, which, for example, is why you can't prove the non-existence of gods. But you can remain highly skeptical about them, given how closely they resemble petulant human beings, and you can demand compelling proof of their existence. Likewise, you need more to validate your claim that "depression" is a biological disorder than intoning, "One day we will surely have proof." You need not add any non-scientific label to what your creative client is presenting, which both on the face of it and after examination looks like despair.

That long, incomplete list of causes of your creative client's sadness is completely sufficient to explain why he is sad. What can possibly help with what's troubling him? Well, many things. We could go down that list and pinpoint exactly how we might want to help him. For his lack of success, we might want to help him become successful. This doesn't sound like a psychotherapist's job, but it is certainly a humane helper's job since that is one sort of help that he needs. We can help him better deal with criticism and rejection so that when it happens again, which it inevitably will, it will sadden him less. We can help him get to his creative work more often, so that he is no longer saddened by his lack of effort. And so on. This isn't so arcane or mysterious. Certain things sadden him; we endeavor to help with each one.

Many things can help. But one of those many things is by far the most important—and it is one that he has direct control over. We can help him get a grip on his own mind. Philosophers from the Buddha to Marcus Aurelius have announced the extent to which this is a top priority. Cognitive-behavioral therapy (CBT) is the modern way that this age-old message is delivered. Almost everyone knows a little bit about cognitive-behavioral therapy and many people have worked with a CB therapist. Why is CBT so popular, so popular that CBT is the primary therapy provided by the United Kingdom's National Health Service? Because its central message is indubitably true: you are what you think.

However, the ways that you are invited to get a grip on your mind, whether those invitations come from traditions like Stoicism or Buddhism or from cognitive-behavioral therapists, are a bit on the dull and unimaginative side. Sit there and meditate? Block a thought and substitute another thought? How playful or inspired is that? As a smart, creative, imaginative person, your client deserves more interesting—and more potent—tactics than those. This book presents sixty of them, based on twin concepts of *dynamic self-regulation* and *healthy indwelling*. Toward that end, I'll introduce the metaphor of "the room that is your mind" and explain how you can use that potent metaphor with clients.

A major shortcoming of cognitive-behavioral therapy is that it doesn't speak to what it feels like to have a mind. We don't just "have thoughts." We keenly experience what it feels like to dwell in our mind. It is sometimes a comfortable place and sometimes a tortured place where we spend much of our waking and sleeping hours. Descartes pictured it as a stage where we play out our dramas. Most people experience that "place that is our mind" as located in the brain: our mind feels located above and behind our eyes. That—and not San Francisco, London, or Berlin—is where we live.

Rather than dubbing your mind a place, I'm designating it a room. That "room that is your mind" turns out to be a room that you can decorate, air out, furnish, and much more. Indeed, you must make that room as friendly and comfortable a place as possible if you want emotional health and a creative life. By making use of the sixty cognitive strategies I'll present, your smart, sensitive, creative clients can finally stop pestering themselves, they can lose that low-grade case of the blues, and they can upgrade their formed personality to become the person they always meant to be. Each strategy addresses a particular problem and the sixty together will help your clients enter into a new and much improved relationship with their own mind.

And this work may prove really enjoyable for them as well! These strategies are a little absurd, a little tongue-in-cheek, a little Alice in Wonderland, and perfectly suited for a smart, sensitive, creative person. They will help them live a less fretful, less claustrophobic, more creative, all around improved life. If your client can put even one of them into practice, it might transform his or her life. And at the same time, they may make your clients smile a little.

Shouldn't they have a little fun as they heal, grow, and change? Indeed, they should! Let's move on now to one of the two concepts I mentioned above, the idea of dynamic self-regulation.

2 Dynamic Self-Regulation

A brain's true brilliance is its ability to chat with itself, enter into self-conversation, and as a result of these conversations engage in dynamic, system-wide self-regulation. Is anything in the universe more amazing than that? Nor is any brain feature more important to you personally or to your clients, since this dynamic self-regulation is the brain feature that allows for mental health and emotional wellbeing.

There are countless ways of thinking about human nature and what really makes us tick. One way is that we are biological machines controlled by our genes, our hormones, our nervous system, and other aspects of biology. When, for example, we sustain a brain injury and lose our memory, that is one sort of proof or evidence that we are our biology. Much less explicitly than you might imagine, this is the predominant view today with respect to mental health. The "medical model" view is that we are mentally healthy when our biology is functioning and we are mentally unwell when our biology fails to function properly. In this view, we should treat mental distress as a biological matter requiring medical treatment, primarily medication.

A second way to think about human nature is that we are primarily psychological creatures who are more or less held hostage by the way our brain, acting as and experienced as our mind, develops, makes sense of our experiences and our circumstances, and manages our desires and our instincts. In this view, we are mentally healthy when our mind refrains from distorting reality, creating unnecessary inner conflicts, succumbing to emotional cravings, and so on—when, that is, it serves us rather than weakens us, harms us or tyrannizes us. This view underpins psychotherapy, which is the second dominant mental health paradigm after the medical model paradigm.

A third way of looking at human nature is that we are this thing called personality, that we are from birth or become over time a formed creature who reacts repetitively and rather without thinking in ways consonant with our genetic predispositions, the lessons we learn from our lived experiences, and our many diverse self-identity pieces. Each person is identifiable as fundamentally himself or herself. In common parlance, we describe people as introverts or extroverts, bubbly or melancholy, rigid or reckless, conventional or iconoclastic, or, in mental disorder language, passive-aggressive, borderline, and so forth. What's implied by these designations is the idea that "everything comes together" as personality, making each of us a predictable, recognizable and rather intractable unity.

A fourth way of describing human nature is by asserting that, fundamentally and above all else, we human beings are social creatures defined by our social roles, social interactions, and relationships. In this view, phenomena like "mob mentality," "authoritarian acquiescence," and "family conflict" reveal our true nature and put the lie to the idea that we are independent actors. In their different ways, family therapy and social therapy both champion this idea by, to take one example, seeing every "problem child" as a family problem. In this view, individual mental health is necessarily contextual and inseparable from family dynamics, group dynamics, interpersonal relationships, and social life. Social psychology is the branch of psychology most curious about these matters—and their experiments are rather convincing in supporting the idea that individuals are much more like herd animals than people might like to imagine.

A fifth view, rather ignored by psychology and psychiatry, is that we are embedded creatures whose circumstances matter much more than we are typically willing to admit. It matters if we must go to a school where we feel unsafe and where we're bullied mercilessly; it matters if we resent and don't like our mate; it matters if we must toil fifty hours a week at a menial job or a high-pressure job. In short, circumstances matter and dramatically affect our mental health. In this view, which I think ought to strike you as common sense, you would expect a homeless refugee to be "anxious" and "depressed," a marginalized youth to be "oppositional" and "defiant," and so on. Any reasonable mental health model must naturally take a person's circumstances into account.

What each of these five views has in common is a rather stark failure to picture human beings as possessing a real mind of the sort that human beings actually have. These models on the whole tend not to credit human beings with the ability to chat with themselves about life, actively make sense of their instincts, desires, psychological workings, and personality, or realize that there are efforts they might make to help with their sadness, anxiety, and other mental health challenges. This is such an odd failure, really, to forget or ignore the fact that human beings are able to chat with themselves about what's going on. Indeed, how could something like psychotherapy possibly work if we didn't have a mind that was able to comprehend, if we didn't possess self-awareness, or if we were just a collection of biological functions, unmediated urges, blind spots, and unconscious processes?

This is a sixth view, then, that we are dynamic, self-regulating organisms that, to put it colloquially, can chat with ourselves and aim ourselves in one direction versus another, toward, for example, calmness versus anxiousness, passion versus indifference, love versus enmity, and so on. We may often do a poor job of dynamic self-regulation, indulge ourselves in thoughts and behaviors that don't serve us, and actually prefer to think that we can't self-regulate. However, that's a shame and not an argument against the reality of self-regulation. We may be some impossible-to-deconstruct conglomeration of drives, appetites, thoughts, feelings, memories, neural events, and everything else human, but what we are *in addition* to all that is a conscious being who knows things, understands things, and can try out things so as to help our situation improve.

Let's imagine how these six models might intersect. You are drinking too much. Your cells are adapting to your drinking habits and now crave alcohol. You certainly have a "biological" problem (and you may have had a biological predisposition to begin with). Your mind likewise craves the alcohol. You now have a "psychological issue" with respect to drinking. You also self-identify as a hard-drinking, passionate artist type and see your drinking as a personality fit. Your "personality" helps sustain the problem. In addition, most of the adults in your family love to drink and you are caught up in a social dynamic that supports your drinking. On top of all that, your job is stressful and your marriage is on the rocks and you drink to relieve those stresses. It's abundantly clear how all five—biology, psychology, personality, social pressures, and circumstances—contribute to your problem drinking.

But here's the human-sized miracle available to you. Through dynamic self-regulation, simply by having a certain sort of chat with yourself, you can from one minute to the next stop drinking—*despite the powerful nature of those five intersecting challenges*. You can enter into what is commonly called recovery, which is essentially an ongoing self-conversation about why you intend not to drink. There is a "you" that wants to drink but there is also a "you" that knows better—and that latter "you" actively thinks, observes, reflects, counter-argues and maintains an ongoing internal conversation in the service of sobriety. Without that dynamic self-regulation piece, sobriety simply isn't happening. By virtue of it, sobriety becomes a reality.

This is so important. *Those five views were influential but not determinative.* Isn't it to your great benefit to remember that this is possible and that this power of dynamic self-regulation is available to you and to your clients? And really, isn't this the best way to picture a human being, not as a strictly biological creature, not as a strictly psychological creature, not as a strictly personality-defined creature, not as a strictly socially compelled creature, and not as a creature who is completely at the mercy of his or her circumstances, but rather as a creature who, through self-conversation, can *figure things out*?

This is a decision that you get to make, both as a person and as a humane helper, to view yourself and others in this way. You can learn how to engage in useful and powerful self-conversation and you can help your clients engage in similarly useful and powerful self-conversations. This view honors the reality of our capacity to think and constitutes our best path to mental health and emotional wellbeing. A dynamic self-regulation model of this sort does not reject the biological, psychological, personality, social, and circumstantial causes of mental and emotional distress. Rather, it rejects a reduced, inaccurate view of human beings as just their biology, just their psychology, just their personality, just their social interactions, or just their circumstances.

A dynamic self-relationship model takes the most into account and, as a result, provides you and your clients with the best chance to achieve mental health and emotional wellbeing. My goal in this book is to help you explore the ins and outs of this dynamic self-regulation process by employing the playful metaphor of a "room that is your mind" where, seated comfortably in your easy chair, you learn how to reduce your sadness, halt pestering thoughts, calm your nerves, eliminate unnecessary dramas, and in other ways radically improve your mental landscape. This dynamic self-regulation is your brain's true brilliance—and it's in your power to choose it as your way of being and to help clients choose it as theirs. If you do, you will have done yourself and them a giant mental health favor.

3 Healthy Indwelling

It is commonplace to have a thought like "It's getting late and I need to leave now." We have millions of these. They do not feel like the result of some inner dialogue, conversation or argument. Rather, they feel exactly like those millions of simple, everyday thoughts that arise in all the ways that thoughts arise, from instinct ("I sure am hungry"), from associations ("That blue is so like the color of my first car!"), from annoyance ("Can't he stop slamming the screen door?"), from fear ("He's driving too fast!"), from sensing and appraising ("This café is very crowded"), from our inner to-do list ("Time to do the dishes!"), and so on. There isn't anything very remarkable there.

Or is there?

Why is it that we hear some of these clearly, some in a muffled and indistinct way, and some in such a whisper that we hardly experience hearing them at all and maybe don't actually quite hear them? Why do some of these everyday thoughts fly in the face of what we know we need to do or what we know we ought to do? The fact of the matter is that many thoughts that appear on the surface simple and that seem as if they ought to be taken at face value have arisen for all sorts of complicated reasons having to do with our half-secret agendas, our defensive maneuvers, our network of biases and prejudices, and for other shadowy, complicated reasons.

A simple, objective-sounding thought, for example "This café is crowded," may prove to be the complicated culmination of an internal conversation of which the thinker is only half-aware or is perhaps even entirely unaware. Say that the thought, "This café is crowded," is thought by a writer who is struggling to write his novel, who doubts his ability to write his novel, who isn't equal to the messy process of writing a novel, and who most of the time finds reasons not to write his novel. For him, the thought "This café is crowded" is not really a bit of objective appraising but rather an excuse to not sit down and write.

He thinks that thought and feels justified in leaving instantly. When he gets to the next café, the thought that arises might be "This café is noisy," which will have arisen for the same reasons. When he gets to the third café, the thought might be, "Oh, I know too many people here and that would prove so distracting!", once again thought for precisely the same reasons, that he is unwilling to face his novel. Soon he's likely to begin drinking instead of writing, hunting for sex instead of for answers to his novel's plot problems, and, by the end of such a day, to feel anger, at himself or at the world, or despair, or both. Yet each of those thoughts sounded so plausible and innocuous!

For most people, these discussions and conversations regularly go on in the dark, in ways that have been traditionally described as half-conscious or unconscious. The person is either not privy to the conversation and is only privy to the resulting thought ("This café is very crowded"); or is perhaps half-aware of the conversation but not so aware of it as to be able to refute it with a counter-thought ("Yes, but I am still sitting down and writing!") For your client to make those hidden or half-hidden conversations known to himself, he will need to turn on a light in the darkened room that is his mind and, with the light on, bravely deal with what he finds. This activity of forthrightly dealing with one's inner reality in a now brightly lit room is what I am calling *healthy indwelling*. Healthy indwelling is the number one self-regulatory tool that human beings possess.

If we better understood how to help clients achieve this healthy indwelling we would surely arrive at new, improved ways of thinking about those things currently called mania, depression, obsession, compulsion, psychosis, post-traumatic stress disorder, attention deficit disorder, and so on. Isn't it reasonable to suppose that states of being and phenomena like despair, guilt or even hearing voices might be the result of, on the one hand, a person's refusal to indwell or, on the other hand, a person's unhealthy indwelling style? If that indeed happens to be the case, then a better understanding of healthy indwelling and more insight into what increases healthy indwelling would amount to huge mental health breakthroughs.

We've long possessed concepts like consciousness, ego, self, mind, awareness, and so on. But, surprisingly enough, given how our understanding of mental health must rise or fall on it, we haven't much explored how each unique person experiences his or her own mind. What is it like when little Johnny or little Mary is "in" his or her own mind? What is it like when adult John and adult Mary find themselves internally musing, fighting, problem-solving, obsessing, and all the rest? What exactly would we see if we could visit John's mind or Mary's mind and could spend time with them there in the "room" that is their mind? Wouldn't that give us the very best understanding possible of John or Mary's motives and difficulties?

What would that inner space look like and feel like? Let's begin to employ the metaphor that we'll use throughout this book, the metaphor of "a room that is your mind," and picture that inner space as a literal as well as a figurative space. Conceptualizing it as a room, we can begin to wonder if it would have windows and feel spacious or prove windowless and feel cramped. Would the walls feel like they were closing in, putting pressure on John to, for example, behave impulsively or indulge an addiction? Since this is the place where John plots his revenge, envisions great success, puts on his superhero cape, re-experiences his pitiful humanness, and all the rest, wouldn't it necessarily feel like quite a dramatic, dynamic place? But what sort of place would it feel like exactly?

Isn't it probably the case that for most people that room is experienced more like a prison cell than a comfy studio by the sea? Picture a person locked in a small prison cell in self-pestering, unpleasant conversation with himself. Cognitive therapy (and all therapy, really) is concerned with what he is saying. However, at least as important is the fact *that he is there*. The room that is a person's mind is not an optional accessory to life. It is the way that human consciousness is experienced. Therefore, as humane helpers we are obliged to concern ourselves with its specific features, features like its airlessness or its breeziness, its spaciousness or its sense of confinement, and so on. We must concern ourselves with these aspects of consciousness at least as much as we concern ourselves with the linguistic bits—the thoughts—that result from that indwelling.

The exercises that I'll be presenting positively affect the size, shape, and dynamics of that room—which in turn will improve the linguistic bits that arise there. The exact analogy is that if we give a room a bright, fresh coat of paint we are then safe in betting that the person living in that room will experience at least a bit of an improved mood. If we conceptualize the mind as a room and picture human beings as often avoiding visiting there, so as to keep their secrets out of conscious awareness, and also regularly visiting there and indwelling intensely, dramatically and often unhappily, that provides us with a more accurate picture of how human beings actually are and what causes so much of their misery.

It isn't just that John may be creating "negative thoughts" or that "thoughts create suffering." It is that our mind is both a place that we avoid, even as worries simmer there and conflicts are fought there, and a place that we painfully inhabit without the ways and means to improve our indwelling. Therefore, we suffer on two scores: that the misery is often going on undetected (and therefore uninterrupted) and that it is exacerbated by our indwelling style—by our lack of enough "mind artistry" to alter or improve the dynamics occurring in that room.

This means that humane helpers have two specific jobs: to help their clients find the courage to enter that room, so that they can hear, interrupt, and deal with those unheard conversations that are not serving them; and that, when in that room, they inhabit it in ways that do the better job of promoting whatever they believe to be important in life: life purpose alignment, contentment, increased creativity and productivity, mental health, and so on.

First, clients must be willing to enter the room that is their mind; second, they must know what to do once they are inside. This book is primarily about what they ought to do once they are inside that room. But let's spend a little time thinking about what can help them find the willingness and the courage to forthrightly inhabit the room that is their mind. Toward that end, let's refresh our memory about existentialism.

4 Existential Traditions and Underpinnings

To engage in the healthy indwelling that I began to describe in the last chapter takes personal courage and a sense of personal responsibility. That these are needed should bring to mind existentialism, particularly the post-war French secular existentialism of Jean-Paul Sartre and Albert Camus and its offshoots and descendants, including existential psychotherapy and existential coaching.

That existential thought lost its luster and that existential practitioners are few and far between today compared to, say, cognitive-behavioral therapists, should alert us to a significant problem that we face as humane helpers who would like our clients to practice healthy indwelling. The problem is that we are asking a lot of our clients when we ask them to courageously take personal responsibility for their thoughts and their indwelling style.

The existentialism of Sartre and other secular existentialists is an ambitious philosophy that demands that each human being try his or her darnedest. It begs the individual to make use of that measure of freedom that he possesses, that he look life in the eye and deal with reality, and that he stand tall as an advocate for human dignity. It argues that life, by pairing tremendous ordinariness with tremendous difficulty and by leading to nothing but death, is a cheat; and that human beings must nevertheless cheat the cheater by adopting an indomitable attitude and by making the value-based life purpose choices that their conscience requires that they make. This agenda sets the bar very high and doesn't seem to suit most people.

This taxing, high-minded existentialism pretty much failed to take hold because it is not really to most people's taste. It makes work for them; it pesters them to be moral; it demands that they articulate their life purposes and live them; it alerts them to the likely complete purposelessness of the universe; and it announces that a kind of perpetual rebellion is necessary if they are to live authentically. It trumpets that fitting in will not do and that all those easy pleasures and vices, while nobody's business but your own, still must be judged by you—and found too easy and too unethical. It keeps asserting that you must be a hero—an absurd hero, to be sure, heroically keeping meaning afloat in the face of the void and working hard at the project of your life, even as life cares nothing about your efforts. It sets the bar extremely high—too high for the vast majority of people, existentialists themselves included.

Existentialists themselves usually failed at living with the bar set that awesomely high. They could articulate why the bar ought to be set that high, at the place of personal responsibility and ethical action they called authentic living, but they found it inconveniently difficult to live that mindful, measured, and pure a life. They proved in the living that much of the time our foibles defeat our intellectual understanding of how we ought to live. They proved it by womanizing. They proved it by gambling. They proved it by succumbing to addiction. They proved it by giving in to despair and taking to the sofa. They proved it by rejecting real work and choosing second-rate projects. They saw clearly where they had placed the bar— apparently much too far above them.

It was simply too hard to live as carefully, ethically, and authentically as the tenets of existentialism demanded. The tenets were lovely, albeit in an ice-water sort of way; but the reality was daunting. Therefore, existentialism never really caught on, even though some people still admire it and even though some practitioners still employ it (or pay lip service to it). For a while after the Second World War millions of young people read about it, nodded in agreement with its premises, but drifted away from it because of its rigors. Jobs called; sex called; vision quests called; soccer on Saturday called; stock portfolios called. It was fine to read a little Nietzsche, Sartre and Camus in college—but it seemed sensible to then put that behind you and get on with your daily commute and your evening drinking.

Existentialism didn't countenance an array of things that human beings actually wanted, like permission to be petty and permission to waste vast amounts of time. It didn't condone silent acquiescence to tyranny or the slogan-sized commandments that religions and other authoritarian, dogmatic philosophies provided. It frowned on group allegiances and social frivolity. Existential philosophy acknowledged these desires perhaps more clearly than any other philosophy but then asked people not to indulge them—and people passed on the invitation. Many who passed remained nostalgic for those high ideals and sometimes did a little looking back, maybe by reading *Nausea* or *The Stranger* in the bathroom; but essentially, they passed on the invitation, nostalgia notwithstanding.

People passed for other reasons, too. Not only did existentialism demand that they live an ethically vigilant life where each action was the culmination of an important internal moral debate, but they were also supposed to "transcend" personality and the facts of existence and escape the net in which every human being is entangled. This was not only a lot to ask—it was perhaps unfair and impossible. How were you supposed to not be the person you had developed into? How were you supposed to shrug off illness, war, disaster, and every manner of calamity and constraint and stand tall? How was any of that really doable?

To take one example, people were supposed to transcend pride. But our smartest, most talented people have rarely been able to come close to such maturity. In their relations with each other, Dostoevsky and Tolstoy couldn't. Camus and Sartre couldn't. Freud and Jung couldn't. Picasso and Matisse couldn't. Elton John and Tina Turner couldn't. Scientists haven't, businesspeople haven't, and parents attending a Little League game or a PTA meeting haven't. It turns out that ego, pride and wounded pride aren't snaps to transcend. Where did we ever get the idea that they were?

Or take the matter of appetite. People with large, undeniable and maybe unquenchable appetites—for sex, for peanuts, for experience, for seduction, for fast rides, for competition, for the rush of adrenaline—were supposed to put their appetites in their back pocket and approach life with the measured restraint of an ascetic. Authenticity required that you avoid gluttony, promiscuity, and all the other faces of appetite. Who wanted to give any of that up? Could it even *be* given up?

Or take human energy itself. The existential vision pictures a human being in control of herself, in the sort of high-bar, dynamic self-regulation place I've been describing. But what if you are flying along in a manic way in pursuit of some impossible dream and really don't want to stop and take a measured reckoning? What if you want to act impulsively—intuitively, if you like—and take a pass on some stolid calm that seriously slows you down? It seemed like a choice had to be made between a snail's pace rationality and our very life force—and most people chose pulsation over calculation.

To be fair, many existentialists understood all this. They understood it very well. Each danced the poignant dance of demanding much from human beings while doubting that the effort was possible or even plausible. They doubted and wondered. Why make such a Herculean effort at authenticity when personality hung like a lead weight around your neck and the facts of existence ruined many or even most of your plans? All that wondering and doubting lead to those trademark ideas of existential thought: fear and trembling, nausea, existential anxiety, existential dread and, of course, absurdity.

Starting in the seventeenth century, we experienced four hundred years of the celebration—and inflation—of the individual. Certain amazing ideas bloomed and some even more amazing realities followed. We got individual rights. We got the rise of science and technology. We got the sense that man might get to know himself and his world through the application of self-awareness and scientific method. We got progress on all fronts. A wild, strange euphoria arose: man mattered! But disaster was brewing.

Existential writers as far back as the pre-Socratic Greeks warned that the better we got to know our situation, the closer we would come to a psychological disaster. We would, by pushing back the curtain and looking reality in the eye, stand face-to-face with a reality so cold that the space between the stars would seem warm by comparison. We would get nothing from science except what science could provide. We would get nothing from civil society except what civil society could provide. We would get nothing from the truth except hard truths. Existentialists understood that we would keep losing hope as each new mighty idea, including and especially that individual human beings mattered, came up against its startling limitations.

The more we announced that man mattered, the more we saw that he really didn't. The better we understood that the dinosaurs could be extinguished in the blink of an eye by an asteroid strike or some other natural disaster, the better we understood that we could suffer a similar fate. The better we understood the power of microbes, and even as we worked hard to fight them, the better we understood that something functionally invisible and endlessly prevalent could end our personal journey on any given afternoon. The more science taught us, the more we shrank in size—and shrank back in horror. You could build the largest particle accelerator the world had ever seen and recreate the Big Bang and psychologically speaking you would end up with only more of nothing—*even* more of nothing, if that were possible.

Certain enormous twentieth-century earthquakes cemented this psychological disaster. Hundreds of millions of human beings had been slaughtered before the Nazis' efforts at extermination, but never before had towering piles of bones appeared in darkened movie theaters as newsreel footage. Never before Hiroshima could our species picture with such spectacular clarity the possibility, verging on something like a certainty, that our species might vanish—and even in our own lifetime. These two events, the Holocaust and Hiroshima, were special. They were something like last straws and somewhere deep inside of us they shattered our belief that individual human life mattered.

It is this apprehension of cosmic indifference that secular existentialists faced squarely—and demanded that you face, too. But who wants that daily dose of despair? We had all somehow wagered that well-stocked supermarkets and guaranteed elections would do the trick and protect us from the void. But they didn't. This now hundred-year-long *certainty* that we are throwaways has made life look completely unfunny. We can laugh together over a bottle of wine and make small talk about this and that, adding a kind of cultural laugh track to a very unfunny situation comedy. But in most of our private seconds there is not much laughter. Rather there is a deep, wide, abiding "Why bother?" And who wanted existentialists reminding us of *that*?

As humane helpers, this is the backdrop against which we work. The ideas of dynamic self-regulation and healthy indwelling are essentially existential ideas, because they make the demand that a human being—you, me, and our clients—make an effort. We can expect that most people will not, which is why we do not exaggerate our goals with respect to helping. We hope to help a little and only maybe sometimes help a lot. We announce that existential ideals are still the right ones—that you take as much control as possible of your thoughts, your attitudes, your moods, your behaviors, and your very orientation toward life and marshal your innate freedom in the service of your intentions—but we know that the void is prominent and that the tasks of authenticity are really difficult. I've made the exercises in this book as light-hearted as possible because life, as existentialists know, is anything but.

I've spent an entire chapter on the relationship between secular existentialism and the ideas of dynamic self-regulation and healthy indwelling because that "room that is your mind" is a room where the existential debates I've just described play themselves out. This is where your client wonders if she matters. This is where your client tries to decide whether to act purposefully or to turn on the television. This is where, when she installs windows (as the first exercise suggests that she do), those windows will not only let in a healthy breeze but also provide her with a ringside view of the void. The "room that is your mind" has always been an existential place—I only wanted to make that fact explicit.

5 Unhealthy Indwelling Versus Healthy Indwelling

Your clients already regularly go to that room that is their mind whether or not you invite them to go there. They have been visiting that room, stewing in that room, and creating problems for themselves in that room since birth. Since it's the case that your clients may currently be indwelling in seriously unhealthy ways, it makes sense to wonder if sending them to "live in their head" even more, so as to try to improve their style of indwelling, is really such a good idea.

This is an interesting and pertinent question. Since it's the case that unhealthy indwelling, one characterized by self-pestering, by repetitive and unhealthy obsessions, by the creation of demanding voices, and so on, can't be good for a client, do we really want to send a client "to his head" to spend more time there, even if it's in the service of improving his indwelling experience? I believe that we do, even if there may be risks involved. Let me explain my reasoning.

First let's consider how an unhealthy, debilitating, and even potentially disabling style of indwelling might arise in a person. As a child, a fellow we'll call John not only loves to spend time in his own head, he really isn't very comfortable anywhere else. John has a vivid imagination, dreams up fantasies and stories for himself, draws cartoons of other worlds, and even as a child has precious little use for what he already disparagingly calls "the real world." In that real world, mostly hellish things go on; and those things that aren't hellish strike him as deathly boring. Because he experiences the real world as either hellish or boring, he avoids it as best he can.

John's mother over-praises him and tells him that he is her little genius and destined to change the world. His father belittles him and verbally attacks him. That his mother praises him but does not protect him from his father's verbal abuse is maddening to him: why not protect him a little more and praise him a little less? Because this makes no sense to him—wouldn't you protect the person destined to change the world, if you really meant what you said?—he both despises her and refuses to believe her message, that he is super-worthy. All of her praise helps contribute to nothing but an inferiority complex.

At the same time, he does feel special, since he knows that the stories he tells himself are indeed good and lively, that his cartoons are excellent, and that he has some spark or gift different from his boring little peers. He indwells more, relentlessly hides out, and pays less and less attention to the doings at school or in his family. His sense of agitation, frustration, and sleeplessness mount and in the course of events he builds up an impressive lack of motivation to do his schoolwork, since his schoolwork bores him silly. He starts to almost fail at school, pulling off barely passing grades just so as not to create too much of a storm at home.

He also starts to build up an impressive lack of coping skills, since he hides out so much and interacts so little with his peers; and an impressive lack of decisiveness, since he can turn any issue over in his head a million ways and see everything from too many angles. His grandiosity increases as he fills notebooks up with what he believes to be brilliant cartoons and witty aphorisms and his sense of inferiority increases as he is snickered at more and more by his peers and belittled more and more by his father. He becomes a kind of god-bug: superhuman when he draws cartoons and easy to squash in the real world.

John is a smart, sensitive, creative boy who is regularly belittled, regularly pressed to succeed, told that he is worthless, told that he is special, who spends great stretches of time in his room because the world feels dangerous, because he is awkward around his peers, and because he has gotten into the lifelong habit of staring at his ceiling and thinking obsessively about his fantasy world. This particular pattern of indwelling becomes habitual and it has that pleasant feeling of habit; and at the same time, it feels completely unpleasant, because a part of him knows exactly to what extent he is hiding out and not living.

He has no friends; he has no dates; he shares in nothing that everyone else at school shares in. His indwelling is habitual, comforting, and pleasant up to a point: and at the same time, he feels ruined. Has he already started to hear voices? Maybe. We can surely see some handwriting on the wall and can safely predict that John is already sad (in pseudo-medical language, suffering from "childhood depression"), anxious (in pseudo-medical language, afflicted with an "obsessive-compulsive disorder") and odd. Maybe he isn't hearing voices yet—but isn't he a likely candidate?

When might those voices arrive, if they do arrive? Probably when that internal pressure increases and he experiences life as even more stressful than it currently feels. Let's add significantly more stress to John's life and imagine him finishing high school by the skin of his teeth and then entering into one of two situations known to help produce their share of so-called psychosis: a war and the first year of college.

John, given his sensibilities, is not likely to enlist in wartime; but if he is drafted, doesn't he seem like an excellent candidate for "battle fatigue"? Looking back at the World War II experience, Samuel Paster wrote in the July, 1948 issue of the *Journal of Nervous and Mental Disease*:

The number of patients admitted to army hospitals with neuropsychiatric disorders during the period January 1, 1942 through June 30, 1945 reached approximately 1,000,000. Approximately 7% of these patients were psychotic. Most of the patients who developed psychotic reactions during the last war became incapacitated prior to shipment overseas, often during the period of basic training.

Can't we picture John in boot camp, thrust among "rough youth," yelled at and bullied by drill sergeants, and obsessing about possible horrible injury or death, breaking under that stress and starting to hear voices? But, of course, it is much more likely that he will go off to college than find himself in a war: and it is that stressful first year of college, filled with the dislocation of leaving home, a cramped space filled with roommates, the simultaneous intensity and meaninglessness of his classes, and the odd demand that he pick a major when he has no idea what his life is meant to be about, that produces so many so-called psychotic breaks in college freshmen and sophomores. Can't we feel how John might attempt to cope with the college experience by indwelling even more intensely and unhealthily than usual and by conjuring up voices?

When and if John starts to hear voices, he is likely to end up in a psychiatrist's office or the psychiatric ward of a hospital. We know full well what will happen then. Little or nothing about John's actual lived experience or indwelling style will get investigated, both because John is not up for such an investigation—he is now indwelling so virulently that he is not available for anything much in the real world—and because such investigations are not part of the current pseudo-medical paradigm's routine. John will receive a diagnosis of "schizophrenia" or something similar and be put on chemicals called medication. This is where we must leave John.

Is the picture I'm painting of John's slide indeed what happens in some human beings and a version of unhealthy indwelling? We do not know. But it is surely a reasonable and intuitively sensible possibility and returns us to the original question: does it make good sense to send a pre-psychotic John, or any client whose sadness, anxiety, or other distress is exacerbated by the way he currently indwells, "to his head" to spend even more time there engaged in indwelling? The answer must be a tempered yes, since it is only there, in the room that is their mind, that human beings can make the changes and improvements that amount to mental health. Even if it is dangerous there, it is the only place where mental health can reside.

It is not as if we might invite a person to abstain from consciousness. That can't be the answer. Rather, our hope is that by painting a picture of what healthy indwelling looks like and feels like, our clients will feel better and live better. We can't be afraid to send a client to his head just because his experience of being in his head hasn't served him very well so far. We want that habitual experience to change and to improve and we hope it can change and improve with our help.

One tenet of the paradigm of humane helping, a paradigm I describe in *Humane Helping*, is that forthrightly acknowledging what we don't know is a better policy than acting as if we do know when we in fact don't. It is perhaps impossible to know how exactly indwelling works, when indwelling is the culprit and when indwelling is the cure, or whether it makes perfect sense to invite a given client to engage in the sort of intentional, mindful healthy indwelling I'm proposing. Who could possibly say for sure?

But it seems sensible to suppose that if we can help a person move from unhealthy indwelling—that is, an indwelling style characterized by self-pestering, self-created sadness and anxiety, and so on—to a healthy indwelling style characterized by a reduction in internal pressure, by a new airiness, and by other improvements, that must be a good thing. Human beings are going to inhabit that room whether or not we invite them to do so and they are going to have a dynamic time of it one way or another. With our help, there is a chance that they might have a much better time of it than they are currently experiencing.

6   Driven, Unsatisfied, Happy, and Tortured

In the first chapter I wondered aloud as to whether smart, sensitive, creative individuals were essentially more like other people or essentially different from other people. My feeling is that they are essentially different. They are different for many reasons but the following four are prominent among them.

First, their struggles to retain their individuality, which is often a lifelong struggle, can make the world feel like the less safe place and their mind the safer place to be. The room that is their mind becomes their safe haven and to the world they appear "introverted." In this and in other senses as well they are driven to indwell.

Smart, sensitive, creative folks look to be born stubborn individualists. It is a creative person's individuality that defines her. Most people are conventional and prize conformity. Only some people prize their individuality. Even if she trains herself to hold her tongue, an individualist will already know as a young child that she wasn't built to conform. Looking around her, unable to understand why people are acting so conventionally, starting to feel alienated and like a "stranger in a strange land," she finds herself burdened by this pulsing energy: the fierce need to be herself.

If she is presented with some arbitrary, odd-sounding rule—that she can only play with one of her toys at a time or that God will be offended if she doesn't wear a wig, she will immediately ask, "Why?" If the answer makes no sense to her or if she gets her ears boxed, she will cry "No!", out loud or internally, and begin to grow oppositional. A certain oppositional attitude naturally and inevitably flows from an individualist's adamant effort to reject humbug and to make personal sense of the world.

This oppositional attitude, perhaps suppressed in childhood, is likely to announce itself and assert itself in adolescence and to grow as an individual's interactions with the conventional world increase. It grows as his ability to "do his thing" is directly or indirectly restricted by the machinery of society. He finds himself in an odd kind of fight, not necessarily with any particular person or group of people but with everyone and everything meant to constrain him and reduce him to a cipher. He finds himself in a fight to the death, a fight to retain his individuality.

One proof that this dynamic actually takes place is the astounding frequency with which we see it in the lives of creative people. Arnold Ludwig, in his study of "1000 extraordinary men and women" called *The Price of Greatness*, explained:

> These individuals often have an attitude set that is oppositional in nature. These are not people who just see that the emperor has no clothes; they offer their own brand of attire for him to wear. When dominant ideologies challenge reason, they feel obliged to speak out, do what they believe is right, and pursue their own goals, even when they may be punished for doing so.

It isn't just that these individualists are having certain thoughts; that would make this a merely cognitive matter in the sense in which one talks about cognitive-behavioral therapy. No, for many it is that they have gone inside and live there, in constant conversation with themselves, and their very lifestyle, no matter what it looks like on the outside—whether they live in a hovel or a mansion, whether they live alone or in a large family—is one of living inside, condemned, as it were, to a life that is something like monologue and something like dialogue and whose atmosphere is that of a windowless cell.

Popping out of the womb individual, needing to experiment and to take risks as part of their individuality, and feeling thwarted and frustrated by the oh-so-conventional universe into which they have been plopped at birth, they rush headlong, like a ski jumper down a ramp, toward reckless ways of dealing with their feelings of alienation and frustration. They are not only individual, they are driven to *be* individual, a drive that sets them apart and sends them racing through life. One consequence of this is to indwell for safety's sake.

Second, nature looks to have invested this group with extra drive. As a group, these individualists have more energy, more charisma, bigger appetites, stronger needs, greater passion, more aliveness, and more avidity. This is no doubt nature's way of fueling the individual so that he can *be* individual. And while nature does not joke it does produce unintended consequences. One of the major unfortunate consequences of this extra drive—this extra ambition, this extra egotism, and this extra appetite—is that individualists are hard-pressed, and often completely unable, to feel satisfied.

Our individualist eats a hundred peanuts—not satisfying enough. He writes a good book—not satisfying enough. He has a shot of excellent Scotch—not satisfying enough. He wins the Nobel Prize—not satisfying enough. This inability to get satisfied produces constant background unhappiness and makes him want some experience that will mask this feeling or make it go away. So he has another hundred peanuts or another Scotch without, however, coming any closer to satisfying himself. This means that while he is indwelling, and even if he is happy with how his mind is working while he is indwelling, he is likely at the same time to feel relentlessly unsatisfied.

Individualists indwell for safety's sake; while there, they are regularly unsatisfied. Third, they possess a qualitatively different mind. It must be the case that differences in intelligence, creativity, and sensitivity produce different minds. We do not need to know what intelligence exactly is to feel safe in saying that Einstein, Picasso, and Virginia Woolf indwell more frequently than do other people, indwell completely differently from other people, and very often indwell happily as they engage in the real work of thinking and creating.

Not only do they visit the room that is their mind much more frequently than do other people, because it is a safe haven and their true home, but while there they engage in very complicated brain activities, holding all that they know in such a way that, for example, a previously unknown relationship among matter, energy, and the speed of light is revealed or whole paragraphs of beautiful prose arrive. These activities frequently make them exquisitely happy, if only for seconds at a time.

While the average person is "thinking of nothing in particular," our smart, sensitive, creative client is busily and intensely indwelling in the service of her creative, intellectual, existential, and moral needs. To my mind, this makes the two groups functionally different, the one group intensely, purposefully, and often obsessively indwelling from birth while the second group is more socially-oriented, extroverted, conventional and, often enough, frankly anti-intellectual.

Fourth, because this group of smart, sensitive, creative individuals has the brainpower to create scientific theories and symphonies, they also have the brainpower to pester themselves in really imaginative ways. They can talk themselves in and out of the belief that they and their efforts matter; they can analyze and over-analyze their motives, the quality of their relationships, and everything else under the sun; they can succumb to seductions created by their ability to romanticize and inflate; and in other ways torture themselves by virtue having a certain neuronal and constitutional endowment.

So nature creates an individual who must know for himself, follow his own path, and be himself, puts it in his mind that he is born to do earth-shattering and life-saving work, gives him the energy to pursue this work and the courage to stand in opposition even to the whole world, and then turns around and lets him torture himself as he indwells. It heightens his core anxiety by giving him an existential outlook, making sure that nothing will satisfy him, pouring adrenaline through his system, and swelling his head so that he is primed to tip over, top-heavy, into self-centeredness.

The combination of a mandate to individuality and a lively brain forces the creative person to wonder about life's largest questions—pesters him with those questions—and demands that he respond to what he sees going on in the universe. It forces him to write a mournful poem, craft a subversive novel, and walk the earth from one end to the other on unnameable quests.

Each of these is an existential response arising from his plaintive, poignant questioning of the world into which nature has dropped him. On top of everything else, nature tells him that he is responsible for looking out for the world—nothing less is expected of him.

This is by no means a complete picture of the reasons why smart, sensitive, creative people indwell as often as they do, the pressures and challenges they experience as they indwell, or the nature, quality, and style of their indwelling. But it is a beginning picture that can help us understand some of the ways in which that indwelling is experienced as sometimes unhealthy and sometimes healthy. What would help make that indwelling healthier much more often? Let's take a look.

7 Keys to Healthy Indwelling

What we are hoping clients can begin to do and continue to do is inhabit the room that is their mind in healthy, productive ways. We want them to visit there of their own volition, rather than being driven there, and we want them to be as happy as possible while they are there, rather than tortured and unhappy.

Of course they will sometimes be driven there, by the pressure of an obsession, by the pressing need for a safe haven, by the demands of their racing brain, and for many other reasons. Likewise they will not always be happy there, not when the novel they are writing is recalcitrant, not when some whiff of meaninglessness fills their nostrils, not when they are brooding about their mate's affairs, and many other times as well. But these are still the high-bar goals that we as humane helpers are promoting: that more often than not they visit of their own volition and that more often than not they are calm, content, and self-friendly as they visit.

What are the keys to achieving these goals? Let me present them from the point of view of a client who has achieved them. The following is where we hope a client may arrive.

1 "I understand the difference between thinking and indwelling. Both are metaphors for complex processes. Metaphorically, thinking is something my brain does and indwelling is something that I do. Indwelling is 'me' in relationship with myself and in conversation with myself. It is the 'place that I go' to self-regulate and the place that I go to 'do my thinking.' Envisioning it as a literal place that I go to, 'the room that is my mind,' has many advantages and can provide me with many benefits."

2 "I can mindfully create this 'room that is my mind' where I go to engage in thinking, musing, creating, fantasizing, problem-solving, and all matters mental. I can design it, I can make decisions about how I will be when I am there (for instance, calm), I can take charge of it, I can decorate it, and I can make it as useful and fanciful as I like. I understand that this metaphor is at once serious and playful, serious in the sense that it allows for improved self-regulation and a healthier internal mental environment, playful in the sense that I can

be as whimsical and imaginative as I like in the way that I design it and use it."

3   "I understand that while I get to go to that room of my own volition, many times I will be driven there by all sorts of pressures. Even if I am driven there, I can still maintain a grip on my mind, still engage in self-regulation, still have the conversations I want and need to have, and still remain an alert presence. If, say, I am driven there by an unproductive obsession, I will learn how to interrupt that obsession as quickly as is humanly possible. I understand that my ability to maintain a perfect internal mental environment is not possible but I will put in place as many strategies and systems as I can so as to create healthy indwelling."

4   "I understand that what's important is not just 'what I think' but the relationship I fashion with my own indwelling. For instance, I want to experience indwelling as if I were sitting in a comfy easy chair rather than lying on a bed of nails. I want to experience indwelling as pressure-free rather than pressurized. I want to experience indwelling as airy and breezy rather than stuffy and stale. All of this I can learn to do!"

5   "While I am there, I can strike an excellent balance between dynamic indwelling and hard thinking about difficult matters, on the one hand, and dreamy relaxation as, for example, when I watch a movie or play a word-game puzzle. Maybe that looks like an hour of intense thinking about my novel followed by an hour of watching a comedy. Maybe that looks like problem-solving how to help my ailing parents followed by a daydream about my European vacation. Each involves the use of my brain, each are instances of indwelling, but I understand that they are different and that it would be wise of me to strike a balance between intense, dynamic indwelling and dreamy, relaxing indwelling.

6   "I can distinguish between healthy indwelling and unhealthy indwelling. To paraphrase the famous opening to Tolstoy's *Anna Karenina*, there's one sort of healthy indwelling and many sorts of unhealthy indwelling, some characterized by too much noise, some characterized by too much ambient sadness, some characterized by too much pressure, some characterized by unproductive obsessions, and so on. I know all these unhealthy versions all too well and I am learning how to deal with each one of them and how to angle myself toward healthy indwelling."

7   "I can sense when indwelling is becoming dangerous and I know what to do when that happens. First, I want to announce in a way that I can hear it, 'This is getting dangerous!' Maybe I can tell that my brain is racing toward an unmediated mania. Maybe I recognize that I've been unproductively obsessing and have crossed over into a very dark place. Maybe my mood is plummeting because of how I'm indwelling. In each of these instances I will announce in a very clear, compelling way, 'This is dangerous' and either change the quality of my indwelling, using the tactics and strategies I'm learning, or else temporarily cease indwelling by doing something like hammering a nail, talking to a friend, playing

with my dog, or singing opera. If my indwelling turns unhealthy, I will take that fact seriously."

8   "I will be careful not to let competing metaphors and competing practices make me forget the central importance of healthy indwelling. For instance, the goals and language of meditation, mindfulness, detachment, and many other potentially beneficial practices may sometimes run counter to and even contradict what I'm trying to accomplish by healthy indwelling. Would I rather be an accomplished meditator or an expert in healthy indwelling? The latter!"

9   "Just as I can arrive at the room that is my mind of my own volition, I can also leave it of my own volition. I understand that part of healthy indwelling is recognizing that I can overdo spending time in the room that is my mind and that what may be required is leaving. Maybe, even though I understand the principles of healthy indwelling, I am nevertheless brooding too much, straining too hard to come up with an answer, overthinking an issue, or creating so many agitating thoughts that they are buzzing like gnats around the easy chair that I've installed. There are countless reasons why I might have to leave—and I am learning how to do so easily."

10   "I understand that thinking is both a process and a relationship. On the one hand, it is the brain working and neurons firing. On the other hand, it is the way that I chat with myself, regulate myself, and serve my interests, especially including those interests I have in living my life purpose choices, creating the psychological experience of meaning, and doing my intellectual and creative work. I am conceptualizing that relationship as taking place in the room that is my mind, where I go to sit in my easy chair to reflect, think hard, problem-solve, muse, commiserate with myself, remember, and all the rest. I may not always be happy there—but I am often happy there and proud to be using my brain in this healthy, helpful and useful way."

The better clients can conceptualize healthy indwelling, the more likely they are to want it and to achieve it. The exercises in Parts II and III support this intention and will help your clients create a right relationship to indwelling and the best environment for healthy indwelling. I also hope that the exercises are light-hearted, charming and imaginative enough to make them smile a little and to hold their interest. Next, let's take a look at how you can use these exercises in your work with your smart, sensitive, and creative clients.

8 Using the Exercises

The exercises that follow in Parts II and III are intended to help your smart, sensitive and creative clients—or any client, for that matter—do a better job of self-regulation, create a healthier indwelling environment and style, and reduce their distress, whatever that distress might be, whether sadness, anxiety, or anything else. Part II offers general help and Part III offers help specifically designed to meet the concerns and challenges of creative clients.

You may want to jump ahead and glance quickly at a few of the exercises from each part, so that you get a sense I what I'm providing. Once you've had a chance to do that, here are some points to consider:

- Each exercise addresses the end-user, your client. In this part, Part I, I am speaking to you, the helper. In Parts II and III, I am speaking directly to clients. Of course, I may also be speaking to you in Parts II and III, if those exercises turn out to serve you as well as your clients.
- Each exercise addresses a particular issue, concern or challenge. However, I think that the benefits of a given exercise go beyond helping with just one issue or concern. For example, if a client manages to install windows in the room that is her mind and maybe for the first time lets a cleansing breeze waft through, who can say what benefits might accrue? If an exercise appeals to you or if you think that it might serve one of your clients, offer it to your client even if your client's challenge isn't precisely the one the exercise is putatively meant to address.
- After I describe the basic set-up—for instance, the rationale for "installing windows in the room that is your mind"—I end each exercise with a number of additional helping questions. These helping questions support the following outcomes: that a client gets in the habit of aligning his thoughts and his behaviors with his intentions, that a client gets to employ his creativity and imagination in the service of solving challenges, and that a client gets to experience large, dramatic change quickly and effortlessly.
- I am presuming that a client will do this work out of session and between sessions. Then a discussion of what transpired as she attempted the work or as she skipped attempting the work can become the centerpiece of the

next session. It is certainly also possible to use the exercises directly in session, by, say, leading a guiding visualization or having the client read the exercise on the spot and by discussing its potential relevance. But since session time is limited and valuable, it may prove wiser to present the exercises as homework for between sessions.

- In order for a client to make use of these exercises, he or she must be able to access them. This means that either you can invite your clients to purchase their own copy of this book or you can print out a particular exercise and provide it to a client. Of course, I think it would serve a client to have access to all the exercises, though naturally a given client may not want to invest in the cost of the book. For that client, presenting the occasional exercise that you print out and that you supply can work well. A third option is to provide clients with their own copy of the book and include the cost of the book in your fee.
- These exercises support the paradigm of humane helping. The two dominant paradigms nowadays with regard to mental health service provision are the pseudo-medical "mental disorder diagnosis and treatment" one, supported by the DSM and ICD, promoted by psychiatry, and generally leading to a chemical fix; and the expert-talk psychotherapy one, where a clinical psychologist, family therapist, mental health counselor, etc., acts as an expert who knows what's going on and maintains a one-up relationship to the clients he sees. A third paradigm, humane helping, which I've described in *Humane Helping* (2017), sees helping as a collaborative enterprise where sufferer and helper are both rather in the dark about what's going on and therefore try out experiments so as to land on solutions that may help the sufferer. The exercises in Parts II and III support that paradigm. As a humane helper, you can't know which, if any, of these exercises will actually help: you are offering them in that spirit, as experiments that may prove useful and not as guaranteed solutions.

The following are some talking points that can help you introduce this material to clients:

- "Whatever is causing your distress, increasing your ability to self-regulate is bound to help."
- "One way to self-regulate is to have useful internal conversations. Where might you have those conversations? Metaphorically, in the room that is your mind."
- "Let's call the experience of visiting that room that is your mind and spending time there *indwelling*. Indwelling can be unhealthy, for instance when you spend your time pestering yourself, bad-mouthing yourself, and so on, or it can be healthy, when you think thoughts that serve you, update your plans so that they match your lived experience, and so on. The sort of indwelling we're after is healthy indwelling."

- "It would be lovely if you could cultivate a mindful, aware indwelling style so that the time you spend in that room that is your mind stops feeling painful and produces much better results."
- "How can you create that healthy indwelling style? The exercises I hope you'll try may go a long way toward answering that question."

Here are some talking points that you can use with clients who are engaging with the exercises:

- "Do you have the experience of your mind as the sort of room the author is describing?"
- "Even if you haven't had that experience, can you visualize such a room and use it the way the author is suggesting?"
- "If you had to describe 'the room that is your mind' in your own words, how would you describe it?
- "What does it feel like to spend time indwelling in your mind?"
- "Would you say that your indwelling style is more a healthy one or more an unhealthy one?"
- "In addition to the author's exercises, what would you like to try so as to improve your experience of indwelling?"

Here are some talking points that you can use with clients whose homework was to work on a particular exercise:

- "I wonder, did you manage to get to the Installing Windows exercise this past week?"
- "One of the points of the Installing Windows exercise was to help you experience a more breezy indwelling. How did that work for you?"
- "The author asked you to do some work aligning your thoughts and your behaviors with your new intentions. How did that work?"
- "The author asked you to do some creative imagining and do the exercise your own way. Did you happen to try that?"
- "Overall, what was the experience like installing windows in the room that is your mind?"

Of course, you might want to try out some of these exercises yourself, either so as to understand better what your clients are attempting or because they speak to you and seem like they might serve you. Since you yourself are no doubt a smart, sensitive, and creative person, these exercises might serve you, too. And who doesn't need to engage in some upgraded self-regulation and some improved indwelling?

You might also like to create some exercises of your own that employ the metaphor of "the room that is your mind." They are fun to create, awaken your imagination, give you a chance to do something both playful and valuable, and allow you to tailor exercises to the needs of your clients and to any special population with whom you may be working. See if producing some exercises of your own might interest you.

It's time to move on to Part II and the first thirty exercises. I hope you find them interesting, provocative, and useful.

Part II
30 Cognitive Strategies for Mental Health

1 Installing Windows

If you look in the mirror, you see your face. But if you look in your mind, what do you see? I think that what you see (or sense) is a windowless room in which something like monologue and something like dialogue take place. I think that you see a room and that you hear your own voice, sometimes asserting ("I want toast!") and sometimes debating ("But isn't wheat bread much better for me than white bread?").

Your mind is a stuffy place, a familiar place, and a troubling place. It is pleasant enough because of its familiarity but troubling because of what you experience there. This is where you doubt. This is where you pine. This is where you announce that nothing is going right. This stuffy, familiar, troubling place is where you dwell in every private moment—and how musty it gets!

It is a place of secrets, secrets that we keep from others and secrets that we keep from ourselves. It is here in this stuffy room that we whisper, fantasize, and get even. This room is occupied in the strangest way: by obvious thoughts like "This jar is hard to open" or "What's on television?" and by strange intimations of that which we do not want to hear and see, like insults not forgotten or the fact of our mortality.

I suspect that every mind would benefit from becoming less windowless. Don't you? Don't you think that just adding windows would help with those things called "depression," "anxiety," "obsessive-compulsive disorder," "mania" and even "schizophrenia"? Isn't it more than stuffy in there: isn't it downright stifling and oppressive? How many times have you thought that thought? How many times have you had that conversation with yourself? How much airless repetition can you possibly tolerate?

What if you installed two windows, threw them open, and let a cross-breeze in? Wouldn't some regrets waft away? Wouldn't some stale conversations dissolve and disappear? Wouldn't you find a little peace without having to travel to the beach or having to open another beer bottle? Wouldn't everything change, just the way that life changes when a cloud passes and we see the sun again? Wouldn't a balmy breeze make you feel altogether better?

The Buddha's phrase "get a grip on your mind" suggests work; and it is indubitably work that cognitive therapists are suggesting when they ask you to engage in thought stopping, thought substituting, and all the rest. Even mindfulness, especially for beginners, is very hard work. But doesn't adding windows and opening them wide sound easy? Doesn't it sound, well, like a breeze?

When I do this easy thing—when I throw open the windows of my mind—I know exactly what benefits I receive. I instantly love more. Maybe it's the imagined gardens, seaside promenades, and quaint villages, maybe it's the children laughing and playing: who can say where the breeze is coming from or where it's going? But I definitely love more with the windows thrown open.

I also think more clearly. I've written more than fifty books and I know what it takes to bring a train of thought to conclusion. It takes showing up, of course; but, having shown up, I do not want claustrophobia. I want airiness, a breeze, and a blue sky. I want concentration, but in a hammock. I want focus, but as in a sea gaze. I want the stillness of a summer afternoon but with the windows open so that sounds can trickle in and the air can keep circulating.

You will love more, think more clearly, feel emotionally better, and maybe even turn any diagnostic label you're saddled with—your "depression" or "post-traumatic stress disorder" or "attention deficit disorder"—into a memory that you can then completely forget as it departs on the next breeze. You don't need screens or storm shutters because you can leave mosquitoes and hurricanes out of the picture: all you need are simple windows that you sometimes shut but that you more often keep open.

Self-mastery isn't only about heavy lifting. It's also about the kind of easy remodeling I'm suggesting. Open windows in the mind do not make you slender, rich, or famous. But they clean house, air the place out, and can make you smile, when, for days, not a single smile has been available. You can imagine those windows; you can open them; they are available. Please add windows to your mind right now, or by tomorrow at the latest, because a windowless mind is a place of serious self-harm.

Primary Issue: Stale, Repetitive, Unproductive Thinking

Additional Issues

Sadness has always been epidemic. Was there ever a time when human beings didn't have reasons to cry? Nowadays this sadness comes with a medical-sounding label and pills are provided. But you might try installing windows and airing out your mind instead. It isn't that a breeze is guaranteed to dispel the blues. But isn't there something poignant and hopeful about throwing open a window, sticking out your head, and feeling the sun on your face? Doesn't that gesture remind you of spring-cleaning and children playing and summer idylls? If sadness dogs your days—or if you've acquired a "clinical depression" label—use this strategy to resurrect hope. Hope is waiting on the next breeze.

Customizing

We once rented a ground-floor apartment in Paris whose tall living room windows opened onto a lovely, quiet Parisian side street. Seated at the table by those windows, eating baguettes and drinking wine, we watched the world go by. The windows installed in my mind are those tall French windows. What sort of windows will you install? I can picture other windows from other times and places: windows looking down on Broadway, windows overlooking bustling Hampstead High Street in London, windows with screens on them looking out onto a lake. Customize this strategy by installing windows that are a little magical and memorable.

5 New Thoughts

Here are five thoughts that support your intention to air out your mind.

1   "Time to let a breeze in!"
2   "I'm spring-cleaning my mind this very afternoon!"
3   "My sadness is a vapor that can just drift away."
4   "A good, stiff breeze will take care of this self-pestering!"
5   "Let me sit by my lovely window and look out at something beautiful."

5 New Behaviors

Here are five behaviors that support your intention to live a less stuffy, less claustrophobic life.

1   When you're feeling anxious, take a moment, picture one of the windows you've installed, slowly open it, stick your head out, and take in a few good deep breaths.
2   Check to see if your physical environment is too dark, stuffy and claustrophobic. If it is, let in some air and some light.
3   A tactic of traditional cognitive-behavioral therapy involves wearing a rubber band and snapping it whenever you hear yourself thinking a thought that doesn't serve you. What if you did that same snapping whenever you noticed that your thinking was too claustrophobic, so as to remind yourself to open a window in your mind?

4   Say that you are about to engage in a behavior that you know you'd prefer avoiding, for example playing yet another video game. What if you make a deal with yourself that you'll hold off playing that video game until you open a window and let your mind air out for two or three minutes? Maybe by the end of those few minutes your need to play that video game will have subsided.

5   Open an actual window. Let in some air. See if that alters and improves your thinking.

Adding Your Brilliance

I've asked you to install windows in your mind to deal with the mental stuffiness that leads to repetitive thinking, chronic self-pestering, and unhappiness. What are your own brilliant solutions to this problem? If you're a painter, might it be interesting to paint a series of windows that let in the afternoon light of a Hopper painting? If that's too literal, what might you try? If you're a software engineer, what's an app solution to the problem of a claustrophobic mind where thoughts fester and sadness grows? If you're a poet, what metaphor might you substitute for my metaphor of window installation? Given that you really need more airiness, what's your brilliant solution to this perennial problem?

Radical Transformation

Let's go a step further. Rather than just installing a few windows, picture your mind as a room with one side completely open to the sea breeze. In that mind of yours, the air is always circulating. In that mind, stuffiness never accumulates. In that mind, new thoughts occur every day and old thoughts just waft away. Your formed personality created a room with no windows; use your available personality to inaugurate a real remodel, one that transforms your mind into a blue-sky place where the heavens can always be seen and where nothing stagnant is permitted. See if you can pull off this radical transformation.

2 Safety Valve

In these lessons, I'm enlisting your native smarts and your creativity and inviting you to better understand how human consciousness actually works and feels. It feels like a place where we dwell and I'm using the metaphor of "the room that is our mind" to capture some of that flavor. In the last chapter, I explained why our mind needs windows and why we must regularly throw those windows open. It can be stuffy to the point of toxicity in that windowless room that is our mind.

Just as dangerously, it can feel like a place of great pressure. It can feel as if we're a hundred leagues under the sea with the weight of all that water squeezing down on us. That windowless room that is our mind is regularly a place of really remarkable pressure. Rarely does it feel like we can just stretch out on a beach chair and sun ourselves. Every so often it can feel that way: maybe when we're holding a smiling baby, maybe when, for a moment, we surrender to the facts of existence and sigh, maybe when, on vacation, we are actually at the beach, sitting in a beach chair, with a cold drink in our hand. But those are the rare moments of mental relaxation.

Most of the rest of the time what we experience in that room that is our mind is pressure, a pressure that makes us race even though we don't want to, that makes us distract ourselves even though we know better, and that can cause us to harm ourselves and to harm others. We've created all sorts of names for that experience of pressure and none of them really captures our felt experience or paints a true enough picture of what's going on.

Take the following example. Say that you're married, off on a business trip, and attracted to someone in the hotel bar. We have words for that like "attraction" and "lust" and "sexual energy" and "instinct" but those words don't capture the pressure put on us by our own mind as our mind begins to do something that, without that pressure, it might well not want to do, namely prepare to betray our mate. We don't just lust but we feel pressured to lust by some unseen imperative.

Take another example. You're a teenager, you've had lots of unsettling and unpleasant experiences, and high school is something like hell. Your mind is a very dark and tumultuous place and, without really being able to explain to yourself why, you find that only cutting yourself with a razor blade helps you release that pressure. Probably you don't exactly call it "pressure"—but if you did, and if you had a way to release that mind pressure in some way other than cutting yourself, wouldn't that be a better way to gain the same relief? Cutting yourself is a too-literal safety valve: wouldn't a figurative safety valve serve you better?

Take a third example. You've always had problems keeping meaning afloat and recently life hasn't been feeling very meaningful to you. Suddenly, out of nowhere, all the meaning drains out of your life. This is a horrible experience; and to deal with that terrible existential pressure you start on a pressurized ill-advised adventure—and become "manic." Wouldn't it be lovely to deal with that pressure in some other way and not have to rush off manically on some wild meaning chase?

Forget for a moment about the exact content of our thoughts in those three situations—thoughts like, "Wow, she is so sexy!", "I hate my life so much!" or "I think I'll build a boat by hand and sail around the world!" A cognitive therapist might want to focus on those words; but I want you to focus on the pressure you're feeling. Who is creating that pressure? That must be you. So, just as you must install windows in your mind and open them regularly to let the must out, it is your job to install a safety valve that you become brilliant at operating and that actually releases that often relentless and sometimes intolerable pressure.

Your mind is a pressure cooker. Therefore, you must fabricate a release valve. That release valve might be as simple as creating and using a mantra like "releasing pressure now," creating and using a more complicated ceremonial safety valve that involves letting the pressure out through your mouth with a "whoosh!", or creating and using a unique strategy that you dream up. If you don't create this release valve and if you don't use it regularly, you will live under that pressure and do things to relieve that pressure that you don't really want to do, like betraying your loved ones, cutting yourself, or racing around in existential despair.

Your first task was to install windows. Now I would like you to create a safety valve that allows you to release all that relentless, recurring mind pressure in a smart, safe way. When you can do that releasing, you will much better manage your mania, your obsessive-compulsive disorder, your addictive behaviors, and all the other consequences that result from not releasing mind pressure soon enough or well enough. Make personal sense of this metaphor of a safety valve and, if you can, do the brilliant thing of creating one right now.

Primary Issue: The Way the Mind Produces Pressure

Additional Issues

What is "obsessive-compulsive disorder" but the playing out of this absurd pressure whose source resides deep within? The same with addiction: isn't the essence of addiction the pressure to drink alcohol, the pressure to gamble, even the pressure to continually check our email? Isn't pressure the driving force behind our addictions? Likewise, isn't mania a pressurized fleeing from something, like meaninglessness, or a pressurized racing toward something, like hoped-for meaning? And anxiety: think of the pressure you experience before an important performance. These unseen pressures drive many, if not most, of the "mental disorders" that plague people. What better help for one of these afflictions than a release valve that reduces or eliminates the pressure!

Customizing

Maybe "pressure cooker" doesn't capture your experience of pressure and maybe therefore "safety valve" isn't the right metaphor for you to employ. What image better captures your experience of the mental pressure that drives you to mischief and distraction? Maybe it's a malfunctioning diving suit or spacesuit? Maybe it's that contraption that crushes cars? Maybe it's a jackhammer? See if you can get clear on what image best represents your particular experience of pressure, then figure out what will help: for instance, a switch that silences the jackhammer or replacing that malfunctioning spacesuit with an intact one?

5 New Thoughts

Here are five thoughts that support your intention to reduce and release mind pressure.

1 "I know how to release this pressure."
2 "I don't have to act just because I feel pressured to act."
3 "Time to use my safety valve!"
4 "Releasing pressure now!"
5 "Whoosh!"

5 New Behaviors

Here are five behaviors that support your intention to release and reduce mind pressure.

1   Choose a small object to carry with you—a special coin, a polished stone—and when you feel that pressure building up in you, take out your coin or stone, rub it as you might rub a talisman, and say, "Releasing pressure now!"

2   Identify some of the stressors that create pressure in your life. See if any of them can be eliminated. For those that can't be eliminated, use your pressure valve to reduce the amount of pressure they produce.

3   Investigate which everyday activities, for example hot showers or walks in nature, serve to reduce your experience of pressure, and make sure to include these activities in your daily routine.

4   See if some change, whether as large as changing careers, as medium-sized as avoiding a toxic family member, or as small as not watching violent television shows before bed, might help to reduce this pressure.

5   Ask yourself the question, "What do I need to do in order to reduce this pressure?" If an answer comes to you, take your own advice.

Adding Your Brilliance

There is no task more important than figuring out how to reduce this unaccountable pressure, since so many of our misadventures and "mental disorders" are fueled by it. Use your brilliance to dream up your own ways of reducing this terrible pressure.

Maybe giving the pressure a name and writing its memoir might fascinate you. If you're a mechanical engineer or a physicist, what might you take away from your knowledge of pressure in the physical world that might prove useful in handling your mental pressure? If you're a singer/songwriter, is there a ballad or anthem to write and sing? Use your brilliance to meet this profound challenge.

Radical Transformation

What is the source of this pressure? Picture yourself traveling deep into your being, through your arteries and your veins on a journey to the source of this terrible pressure. You pass all the superficial rationality, all the usual landmarks, and all the civilized thoughts and measured feelings, and you go deeper into the tangle, roaring through tunnels and dropping precipitously, until you reach … the source. What do you see there, face to face with the source of all this terrible pressure? And can you maybe, just maybe, snap your fingers and banish it forever?

3 Easy Chair

For many of our tasks and challenges in life it's possible to create step-by-step programs. You can create a sensible program for moving your infant from formula to finger foods and take into account realities like watching out for allergies. You can create a diet and exercise program with excellent specificity. But turning your brain brilliant and healthy aren't challenges that allow for such neatness. There isn't a first thing to do, then a second thing, and so on. Rather, there are many separate efforts to make. Each of our exercises tackles a different way in which we harm ourselves and presents a metaphoric solution for that particular problem.

Nevertheless, though there aren't any neat, consecutive steps, something builds as you work these exercises. The exact analogy is working on your personality. You can work on any aspect of your personality, for example making an effort to increase your confidence, your resilience, your calmness, or your passion, and by working on that single aspect you will be upgrading your whole personality. Here, tackling these lessons, you are upgrading the way that you use your mind and the way that you relate to your mind by working on one challenge at a time. The first challenge was mental staleness that traps us in repetitive thinking. The second challenge was mental pressure that drives us to act in ways that harm us. In this chapter, the challenge is the amazing self-unfriendliness that so many people display toward themselves.

Do you see that bed of nails prominently positioned in the middle of the room that is your mind? That bed of nails upon which you deposit yourself roughly each night and upon which you struggle through your afternoon nap, treating yourself terribly uncomfortably so as to remind yourself about all the ways that you've failed yourself and so as to punish yourself for mangling your life? Isn't part of you absolutely certain that you deserve that bed of nails, that you should writhe in pain rather than rest, and that poking yourself with those sharp metal points is the only way to expiate your guilt?

Please stop that.

Get rid of that bed of nails right now. Call in the haulers and get it the heck out. Watch them leave with it. Pay them a little extra to destroy it, so that no one finds it and thinks that they deserve it. Tip the haulers handsomely and thank them profusely. They are carrying out the thing that has harmed you the most, your enduring self-indictment. It is time to sign your pardon. That bed of nails is, and has always been, cruel if not unusual punishment.

Okay! It's been hauled away. Next, go online in your mind's eye and buy yourself exactly the easy chair that you've never permitted yourself. Make sure it's comfortable! Skip that chair-as-art that was never meant to be sat on. Get something comfy. You want an easy chair that is genuinely easy to relax in because that ease is going to translate into better living. Take your time shopping!

Picture where you'll place your easy chair in that room that is your mind. Maybe right beside one of those windows you installed, maybe the one facing that gorgeous view or the one that lets in the most air? Or maybe you'll put it right next to the refrigerator, if impulse snacking isn't a problem for you. Get its placement pictured, make your purchase, have it delivered, and wait expectantly at the door when it's due to arrive. Point the movers to exactly where you want it positioned. Then sit!

Do you deserve that easy chair? Of course, you do. Do you deserve it even though you've made a hash of this and a mash of that? Of course, you do. Do you deserve it even though you were to blame for that terrible A, even though you were the cause of that horrible B, and even though you didn't help when it came to that awful C? Of course, you do. By purchasing it and sitting in it you are announcing that you are human, and that, warts and all, you deserve some ease. By living more easily inside, by relaxing better, by pestering yourself less, by finally getting off that bed of nails, you position yourself for self-improvement. It is easier to be your best you when your mind isn't being jabbed continually.

Your easy chair is your place for relaxation, rejuvenation, daydreams, bursts of imagination, forgiveness, hard thinking, renewed hope, and everything else done better in an easy chair than on a bed of nails. No doubt you agree; and yet it may prove supremely hard to part with your bed of nails. It exists in your mind because for the longest time you've been certain that you deserve it. Part of you is positive that you ought to punish yourself for all those messes, mistakes, and missteps. I'm guessing that it may prove hard to get it into your head that you're not obliged to sleep on that bed of nails.

But you aren't obliged. Really.

To sleep on that bed of nails is only to make matters worse, not better. If you want to expiate your guilt, rise up and do a good deed, say a kind word, make a difference. Is doing any of that made easier by having spent the night tortured on a bed of nails? No, absolutely not. Had you spent a lovely few minutes in an easy chair, you'd be in a much better mood and much better prepared for goodness. Your bed of nails isn't some sort of necessity or your destiny. Please, call the haulers!

Primary Issue: Self-Inflicted Pain and Self-Pestering

Additional Issues

Are you very self-critical? Do you disparage your efforts, even including your undeniable successes? Were you raised in a tradition that added to the problem, one with an emphasis on guilt, sin, and personal wrongdoing, where you were supposed to scrutinize your every move and mostly find yourself wanting? If so, then this exercise is crucial. It is past time to discard that bed of nails and replace it with an easy chair. You may want to focus on this work and not move on to another chapter until you've called the haulers!

Customizing

Maybe a loveseat better suits you than an easy chair? Or maybe it's a rocking chair? Or you could replace that bed of nails with a comfortable bed and high-quality linens. It's also possible that the metaphor of a bed of nails doesn't quite capture the particular way that you criticize, pester and beleaguer yourself. What's the right imagery for you?

5 New Thoughts

Here are five thoughts that support your intention to replace your self-pestering with new lightness and ease.

1   "No bed of nails for me!"
2   "I deserve better from and for myself."
3   "I am worthy."
4   "Lightness and ease."
5   "I am becoming self-friendly."

5 New Behaviors

Here are five behaviors that support your intention to replace your self-pestering with new self-friendly lightness and ease.

1   Begin to notice which of your behaviors seem to come from a self-friendly place and which seem to come from a self-unfriendly place. To begin with, just notice. That's an important first step!
2   Pick one behavior that looks to be coming from that self-unfriendly place. Give yourself the following instruction: "The next time I'm about to behave in this way I'm going to picture that easy chair and see if that makes a difference."

3   When you feel yourself about to behave in that self-unfriendly, self-critical way, picture that bed of nails being hauled away and the arrival of your comfy easy chair. Sit in it for a bit. See if that lovely pause and that bit of ease allow you to avoid behaving in the way you were about to behave.

4   Repeat this process with another behavior that looks to be coming from that same self-unfriendly place. Maybe the first behavior was the way you apologize too much when you speak; now maybe you'll look at your binge eating.

5   Continue the process of identifying and preventing behaviors produced by that bed of nails that, although hauled away, likely hasn't been hauled away quite far enough yet. Each time you manage to prevent one of those behaviors, you're taking another step toward ridding yourself of self-inflicted pain.

Adding Your Brilliance

There are no more important subjects than the ways in which we diminish, derail and defeat ourselves, and inflict pain on ourselves. Turn your brilliance to this subject of self-inflicted pain. You might try asking the question "Why do I do that?" from a new perspective, say from the perspective of an evolutionary biologist or an evolutionary psychologist, hazarding some fascinating guesses about why human beings do all that self-unfriendly self-inflicting. Don't worry if those aren't your fields: try some imaginative guessing. Your guess may be as good as anyone's!

Radical Transformation

How might you become a person who no longer finds it necessary to sleep on that bed of nails? Let's try the surgical removal of self-loathing. Locate that tumor from which flow indictments like "I always screw up" and "I'm really not very good at anything" and "All my critics are exactly right." Have you got it located? Now get out your laser. Carefully remove that tumor with your laser and dispose of the tumor in a toxic waste bag. You are now on your own side. Periodically scan for that tumor's return.

4 Second Answers

Something comes up and you really need an answer. Your mate receives a job offer to work on the other side of the world. Will you accompany her? You have a medical condition that might be treated in any one of three ways. Which treatment will you choose? At such times, do you settle down in the room that is your mind and think? Or, when you go there, do you find that a thought is already waiting for you? "No, I'm not going!" "No, no chemo for me!" And if you find that a thought of that sort is waiting for you, if indeed it pounces on you the moment you enter, how reliable should you consider it? And ... *where did it even come from?*

I once spent a little time studying the reactions of French painters to the commencement of the Franco–Prussian War. The war began. Each painter reacted idiosyncratically. One decided that it might prove valuable artistically to see war and therefore he enlisted. A second shook his head at the madness of war and decided to ignore it completely. A third, wondering about his courage, enlisted to test himself. A fourth fled to the countryside so that he could paint in peace and avoid conscription. A fifth protested the war. A sixth decided to stay home and paint "beautiful things" as a kind of antidote or counterpoint to the horribleness of war, using his parents' connections to avoid conscription. A seventh did nothing, got conscripted, and was killed almost immediately. And so on.

We understand each of these reactions. But more than that, we sense what has gone on in the mind of each of these painters. They heard about the commencement of hostilities—and they reacted. An already-formed thought almost surely greeted them instantly, leaving no room for serious reflection. How many of these painters scoured all of their available choices and tried to decide which made the most sense? Don't you imagine, virtually none? They reacted according to their formed personality, as if they were snapping their fingers. Hence the phrase "snap decision."

This is very interesting and very important. If the "answer" awaits us as we walk in the door, if some analysis or train of thought or spontaneous reaction *has already taken place* before we even enter the room that is our mind, doesn't that enslave us to the murky doings of our unconscious and the straitjacket of our formed personality? And mustn't mastery of ourselves include an awareness that we will meet already-formed answers as soon as we enter and that as powerful and influential as they feel, they must not be considered our final answer? They are at best the starting point of our inquiries; they are absolutely not gospel!

Remember that game show where a contestant would give an answer to a question and then the host would say, "Is that your final answer?" Often the contestant would think again—and almost always repeat his answer, as there was no actual thinking involved, only the accessing of stored information. Either he could remember a name, date or some other fact or he couldn't. For you, however, the answer that is waiting for you mustn't be considered your final answer, since you haven't given the matter any thought yet. When there is an important decision to be made, you want to think and not just react.

Since an automatic answer will be waiting for you and since we are programmed to accept those answers, you will need to have a chat with yourself when you enter that room and find an answer waiting for you. Your chat might sound like: "I didn't arrive at this answer. It was just waiting for me. Since it was already waiting for me, it no doubt reflects some thoughts and feelings I'm having. But maybe it arose out of anxiety, fear, rage, or who knows what. Since it was waiting for me, that makes it too easy an answer and therefore I reject it. Instead of accepting it, I will think. If, upon reflection, I come to the same answer, then I'll trust it more. And if I come to a different answer—well, then thank goodness I checked!"

Doesn't this skepticism about the validity of ideas that are waiting for us throw the whole idea of intuition into question? It does and it should. Intuition, snap judgments, and snap decisions all have their place but they are not to be revered above thinking and they mustn't replace thinking when thinking is required. In retrospect, our life can look like a series of snap decisions—and how well did that work out for you? You have a brilliant brain that would love to assist you. Don't accept its first answers; make it do more work than that.

For the first three exercises, I suggested other issues that the exercise might be used to address, provided you with examples of thoughts and actions that supported the exercise's central intention, and invited you to customize the exercise, add your brilliance, and imagine how a quick, radical transformation might be possible.

For the remaining exercises, I invite you to tackle these additional questions yourself. Tackling them is extremely valuable and will help you learn the art of dynamic self-regulation and healthy indwelling. Here are the questions for you to answer for this exercise and for subsequent exercises as well.

Primary Issue: Relying on Automatic Thinking

- What other issues might this exercise help address?
- How might you personalize and customize this exercise?
- What are five thoughts that would align with and support this exercise's central intention?
- What five actions might you take so as to support any changes you consider important to make?
- How might you use your imagination and your native brilliance to customize this exercise, upgrade your personality, improve your experience of indwelling, or meet the challenge this exercise is addressing?
- Imagine that a quick, radical transformation in the direction suggested by this exercise might be possible. What might that transformation look like?

5 Admonishing Trickster

The trickster is a character out of world folklore. Cultures everywhere have identified this part of our nature. Let's foul the well water. Let's sleep with our neighbor's wife. Let's steal those chickens. Let's do worse. Let's plunder. Let's turn whole communities against one another. Let's make a giant mess of everyone's life. Let's be a trickster!

Where do these sly, nasty, horrible impulses come from that inhabit everyone? Why is each of us such a trickster? Why do we start the day moral, compassionate, and upright and somewhere around noon turn into coyote, ravenous for mischief? Did the world offend us so deeply that we constantly ache for revenge? Did we not get our bottles on time as infants? What made us tricksters?

I vividly remember trickster moments from childhood. Two boys were racing side-by-side in the schoolyard and, out from the crowd lined up on either side, came a foot to trip one of them—my foot. Why? I had nothing against the boy I tripped. I cared nothing about the outcome of the race. In fact, not a thing about those two boys racing mattered to me. So why spoil it for one of them?

In folklore the trickster steals food, steals sex, steals fire, steals whatever he can. He changes shape so that he can't be spotted and can't be caught. Indeed, I've stolen food, most peculiarly during a bizarre, inglorious shoplifting period where all I cared to shoplift was smoked salmon. I've changed shapes from one moment to the next, charming and funny one moment, cold and absent the next, then gregarious, then unapproachable. Haven't you?

Is trickster sitting in a corner of your mind right now, maybe posing as a designer lamp or a postcard from Spain or a half-eaten sandwich? The second you blink there he is, full coyote, wild-eyed, meaner than you imagined, your very own trickster organ, part of you, hungry to damage someone—maybe you. In the room that is your mind, trickster is always around somewhere. Just lift up a corner of the rug or move a can of peas on the shelf. There's trickster!

What can be done to rid your mind of your trickster impulses? Can trickster be caged? Jailed? Banished? Tricked? No, none of that will work. But he can be admonished. You can wag your finger at that part of your nature and say, "That is absolutely not okay, that bit of mischief you're planning." Every time you see trickster, even if he's disguised as half a tuna fish sandwich, you can exclaim, "Absolutely not, trickster. Absolutely not."

You can announce, out loud in that voice you use when you really mean something, that you are on to his tricks, that he isn't the least bit amusing, and that you really, really don't appreciate him. Don't give him an inch— he'll take your whole leg and arm. Don't bestow even the smallest smile on him—he'll take that for full license. He is devious, he is not your friend, and he wants to pull the wool over your eyes. Tell him you know what's he up to!

The room that is our mind is full of shadows. Pulling back the shades and letting in light can help. Turning on a lamp can help. We need more illumination and fewer shadows, more awareness and less impulsiveness. Where do those sly, nasty, downright vicious impulses come from? Who knows! Where do they reside? Right next to us as we read a book, right beside us in bed, right in our mind even as we try to be our civilized best.

Trickster is not your friend. Trickster is no one's friend. His laugh is malicious, his plans are devious, and his desires are unworthy. We tolerate trickster living in our mind because, well, he is who we are. We are part-trickster. We can be that bad boy and that bad girl. We can be that person who would love to trip someone. We can be that person who much prefers a stolen donut to a purchased one. Coyote lives in our mind because evolution invited him.

Right now, visit the room that is your mind. Find trickster. He's somewhere, in the cupboard, in the corner, or sitting right in your own easy chair, laughing at you and daring you to move him. Find him and admonish him. Explain to him that you know him and that you do not cherish him, that you do not find him funny, that you do not want him living in your mind. It doesn't matter that he won't listen, that he'll play a game on you, that he'll change shape and become your socks, that he can't be exterminated. Your job is to notice him and admonish him and let him know—let you know, since you are trickster—that you do not admire him.

Your mind makes all that mischief. Starting today, try to make less.

Primary Issue: Dealing with Our Inclination toward Mischief

What other issues might this exercise help address?

- How might you personalize and customize this exercise?
- What are five thoughts that would align with and support this exercise's central intention?

- What five actions might you take so as to support any changes you consider important to make?
- How might you use your imagination and your native brilliance to customize this exercise, upgrade your personality, improve your experience of indwelling, or meet the challenge this exercise is addressing?
- Imagine that a quick, radical transformation in the direction suggested by this exercise might be possible. What might that transformation look like?

6   Empty Platform

Right now, you are reading this. But maybe it is also raining and you can hear the rain pounding on your roof. Does that make you worry if the roof shingles will hold? And maybe a baby is crying two houses over. Why won't somebody please quiet that baby? And maybe your son went off to school without his permission slip signed—what can be done about that? Will he be forced to miss his field trip and might he never forgive you? And maybe you're just a little bit hungry—or maybe you're very hungry—and that leftover croissant on the kitchen table is beginning to pull at you. Of course, you shouldn't really eat it ... and it doesn't microwave properly anyway ... and on top of that ...

Such is the room that is our mind. It is a place of babel, of competing thoughts and sensations, of flickers of desire and nanoseconds of regret, of pressing singularities and wild simultaneities, of a cacophony of tossing and tumbling! How is anything to be felt deeply or thought about carefully when ... is that the baby crying again? Where *are* his parents! And too bad about that permission slip! And ... wait, what was I saying?

Picture your easy chair, the one you substituted for that nasty bed of nails. Maybe you can make the following deal with yourself. Maybe you can say to yourself, "When I want to feel something deeply, like the time I'm spending with my mate, I will sit myself in my easy chair and not hear that babel. When I'm in my easy chair, I will be completely present." Likewise, when you want to think hard about something, like the direction you want to take your business, you can say to yourself, "When I want to think clearly, I will sit myself in my easy chair. Then I'll think only about my business and not about how overwhelmed I'm feeling or about how I wish my neighbors would take care of their crying baby!"

You can use your easy chair to focus, to become present, and to deal with the roar of simultaneous happenings. In addition, you might try the following. Picture the room that is your mind as a crowded train platform full to the brim with folks waiting for a train to a faraway place. There's tumult everywhere, luggage carts and backpacks and golf clubs and shopping bags filled with provisions for the journey. The train is three minutes away. A flashing sign counts down the minutes. Two minutes to arrival! You can hear the train in the distance. Now it's here! In it roars, sounding its horn to warn passengers back from the edge and producing a whirlwind.

The doors fly open and everyone begins boarding. Everyone boards ... except you. You are not traveling. Instead you sit yourself on one of the vacated benches and watch the train pull out. When it is gone, all is calm. You have the whole platform to yourself. You can think anything you like and feel anything you like without interruption. You have no luggage to watch, no unused ticket to toss, no salami sandwich crying to be eaten. You are sitting in a place of deep silence.

Yes, there's a bit of a chill breeze blowing through the station, some unexplained rumbles, and an echo if you shout. But this is still about as quiet as a mind can get. No doubt new passengers will arrive to board the next train to another faraway place. But they won't show up for a while, not even the earliest of the early birds. For a precious quarter of an hour you can feel deeply, if you like. For half an hour, at least, you can follow some train of thought. Goodbye overnight train to Berlin, au revoir Paris express, I've a train of thought to follow!

Whenever you need to, transform the room that is your mind into an empty train platform where you can stake out a bench, shut your eyes, and shed all that nattering about broken shingles, babies wailing and unsigned permission slips. Hear nothing except the mournful sound of a distant train whistle—and whatever you really mean to be thinking. Tame the noisy, busy now with some precious quiet time, either in your easy chair or on your platform bench. Otherwise you'll mix your budding thoughts about the direction to take your business with weird fragments about crying babies and flying shingles and where will *that* get you!

Primary Issue: Too Many Competing Thoughts and Feelings

- What other issues might this exercise help address?
- How might you personalize and customize this exercise?
- What are five thoughts that would align with and support this exercise's central intention?
- What five actions might you take so as to support any changes you consider important to make?
- How might you use your imagination and your native brilliance to customize this exercise, upgrade your personality, improve your experience of indwelling, or meet the challenge this exercise is addressing?
- Imagine that a quick, radical transformation in the direction suggested by this exercise might be possible. What might that transformation look like?

7 Exit Door

If you've ever found yourself buttonholed by someone who can't stop speaking, whose pressurized speech races on and on and who won't accept any interruption, you know that nothing at all can interfere with that person's agenda, whether that's convincing you that Martians abducted him, vaccinations ought to be made illegal, or that youth today are self-indulgent and worthless.

It won't help to exclaim, "Stop, enough!" It won't help to present some counter-argument. It won't help to roll your eyes or make some "please stop!" gesture with your upraised palm. Your interlocutor is on a mission that has nothing to do with you, a mission to spill out the words that his mind is driving along with a whip.

Were you to exclaim "Stop!" he might actually stop for a split second, give you a look of amazed incredulity, as if to say, "What, you don't think that Martians are everywhere?", and return immediately to his theme. Shake your head if you like; that won't faze him. To free yourself of his manic monologue, you must leave. There is absolutely nothing else to do. You must say, "Oh, I see Mary across the room and I haven't chatted with Mary in the longest time! It was SO nice chatting with you." Then you bolt. Or maybe you skip any politeness, turn your back, and just flee.

Your own mind can be exactly like that. It can get on some bandwagon, usually under the pressure of some unacknowledged threat, for instance that life is feeling meaningless and you don't want to notice that terrible shortfall, and jibber on about some theme that suddenly seems important beyond belief. Maybe it's how the walls are not quite the right shade of white and really must be repainted this instant ("Navajo white, they should be Navajo white!"), how it's imperative that you set off for South America on that quirky adventure that you've delayed thirty years, or how you really must tell your boss off in no uncertain terms this very morning. There your mind goes!

Such monologues are so very hard to interrupt. There appears to be no "you" available at such tense times to say, "Bob, it's not about the walls" or "Calm down, this is not the year to run off to South America" or "Hold on, better to ask for a raise than to spit in his face." It is as if you have ensconced an orator on a platform right in the center of the room that is your mind and you are now obliged to let that speaker orate, no matter what. And if someone dares stand up and shout, "That's just insane!", his retort is ready: "Get that traitor out of here!"

What can you do when your mind is going on like that? Leave the monologue. That's the thing to do! In an earlier exercise, you installed windows in your mind so that fresh air might flow in. Now you must install a door by which you can leave. You need an exit; your mind must not be a "no exit" kind of place. Say to yourself, to the "you" trapped listening to yourself go on and on, "I'm leaving now." Get up, turn your back on that mania, get a firm grip on the doorknob, get your exit door opened, and stride into some sunny, blissful silence.

Once outside, as you walk in silence through a quiet garden in the direction of a café and some tea and biscotti, you might dare to ask yourself, "What was that all about?" You were that manic speaker; your mind produced that feverish monologue; so, no doubt, there is something to learn about why you felt compelled to go on that way. In the blissful silence of that garden walk, dare to quietly ask that poignant question: "What *was* that all about?"

These pressurized monologues arise all the time. Maybe you call them your obsessional thinking or your manic times or maybe you don't have a name for them. Maybe they are just a part of you that you suppose you can't do much about. But there is something you can do, if you would like to gain some freedom from pressure-driven monologues. You can create an exit—maybe with a nice bit of red neon above the door that reads "Exit"— and leave whenever it would be wise for you to get out of there.

Certainly, there are other ways to handle our manic energy, our obsessional thinking, and the crises that bring them on. But isn't just leaving a refreshingly simple one? You quietly get up—no need to remonstrate the speaker, no need to announce your intentions—and leave. Then, there you suddenly are, in the silence of a lovely garden, on your way to an afternoon treat. Make sure that the room that is your mind is equipped with that exit door.

Primary Issue: Obsessive Thinking

- What other issues might this exercise help address?
- How might you personalize and customize this exercise?
- What are five thoughts that would align with and support this exercise's central intention?
- What five actions might you take so as to support any changes you consider important to make?

- How might you use your imagination and your native brilliance to customize this exercise, upgrade your personality, improve your experience of indwelling, or meet the challenge this exercise is addressing?
- Imagine that a quick, radical transformation in the direction suggested by this exercise might be possible. What might that transformation look like?

8   Tantrum Mind

Ever see a three-year-old throw a tantrum? Picture that three-year-old playing some obsessive game. All of his pieces are on the floor and in perfect order. He's consumed and in a trance, telling himself a story about pirates or soldiers or train crashes. You walk by, friendly and amused—and accidentally knock one of his pieces off its mark. A quite amazing tantrum ensues, out of all proportion to that trifling accident.

It's absurd, really, considering that all that's required for perfect order to be restored is that he move that pirate or soldier or train back a few inches and put it in its place. Absurd or not, out of all proportion or not, there it is: a real tantrum that no parent has yet figured out how to soothe or interrupt. That tantrum must just run its course.

That's really not so tragic, even if that tantrum happens in a supermarket and embarrasses you no end. But what about its adult versions? Don't we see foreshadowed in that three-year-old's tantrum road rage, domestic violence, family feuds, and war? There, in its adult versions, the inability to forestall or interrupt a tantrum has massive effects. Whole mobs go into tantrum mode. Whole countries go into tantrum mode. And nothing known to man can stop them until the tantrum runs its course.

We are all susceptible to these tantrums and they make a bit of a mockery of the idea that we are civilized or that we can adequately get a grip on our mind or our emotions. But isn't there in fact a split second—the most micro of microseconds—during which that three-year-old, and adults too, allow themselves the indulgence of the tantrum? Isn't there that briefest of brief moments that, as brief as it is, is nevertheless long enough for that three-year-old to say to himself, "I think I'd like to throw a tantrum now. Here I go!"?

I think we can change our mind in that moment. I think that we can dispute the tantrum. This would sound like, "I am not going to throw a tantrum now." Our mate may for the millionth time leave a dirty thing in the exact wrong place. We could throw a tantrum or we could murmur, "I am not throwing a tantrum now." Are you justified in throwing that tantrum? Who can say. However, does it serve you to throw that tantrum? Almost certainly not. No three-year-old, after the fact, and after some privilege has been withdrawn or some penalty exacted, has ever said to himself, "That tantrum was so worth it." Nor has many an adult.

Sometimes we think, "A tantrum will feel so good!" But does it feel that good? This is a serious question. If tantrums actually made you happy, then that would amount to at least one reason to throw them—and quite likely the only reason, since they never gain us anything or make a positive difference. But do they actually make you happy? Can you really say, "I'm so happy I threw that tantrum at work!" or "I'm so happy I threw that tantrum with my sister!" or "I'm so happy I threw that tantrum with that customer service representative!" Did any of those tantrums make you feel happy?

I think not. But even if they did—even if those absurd, childish explosions provided relief that you experienced as pleasure—even then, it would still be part of your program of dynamic self-regulation and healthy indwelling to put into practice a rejection of tantrums. You have an agenda—brilliant mental health—and the reason you opt for that agenda is so that you can live your life purpose choices and influence the creation of meaning. Every tantrum, however good it may possibly feel, robs you of precious time and precious energy that you could be using to live well.

Experience tells us that even that three-year-old can gain some mastery over those tantrums and can decide that, given the consequences of indulging those tantrums and also given how bad they actually feel, he will stop himself in his tracks. He will not go wild when that pirate, soldier or train is accidentally and unceremoniously moved. Many a three-year-old has come to that conclusion—and so can you.

Each of us has a tantrum mind. It is part of our inheritance and it is rather clear why nature thought that feature might serve us and why it would program our selfish genes to throw a really symphonic fit whenever we didn't get our way. But that genetic selfishness doesn't serve you or me. Let's do better; and in that microsecond before a tantrum is about to erupt, let's say no to it. That outburst you just prevented wasn't going to feel that delicious anyway. Spare yourself the loss of some essential self-worth and simply skip it.

Primary Issue: Overdramatizing and Lack of Impulse Control

- What other issues might this exercise help address?
- How might you personalize and customize this exercise?
- What are five thoughts that would align with and support this exercise's central intention?
- What five actions might you take so as to support any changes you consider important to make?

- How might you use your imagination and your native brilliance to customize this exercise, upgrade your personality, improve your experience of indwelling, or meet the challenge this exercise is addressing?
- Imagine that a quick, radical transformation in the direction suggested by this exercise might be possible. What might that transformation look like?

9 Tactics Table

There you are in the room that is your mind, sitting there … bored. That is a big problem. Boredom breeds mischief. And that mischief, which can produce real messes, only relieves the boredom for a moment. You drive at a hundred miles an hour: as soon as you park, the boredom returns. You engage in the wildest sex: two seconds after orgasm, the boredom returns. Said the nineteenth-century novelist Stendhal, "This is the curse of our age, that even the strangest aberrations are no cure for boredom." Hasn't the problem gotten even worse in this age of trivia?

What to do?

Let's add a tactics table to the furniture in the room that is your mind. Picture the sort of table used in war rooms where military commanders move around their ships or troops and prepare to do battle. Your tactics table has drawers out of which you pull tactics to deal with challenges. The instant you're bored, you pull open the drawer labeled "boredom," you remove the five tiles with reminders engraved on them, you lay them out in front of you, and you prepare to battle boredom.

The first tile reads, "Do not fear boredom." This reminds you that boredom is a psychological state and that it will pass. Experiencing a little boredom is no tragedy and no reason to overthrow your life. Call boredom uncomfortable, disconcerting, but not the end of the world. Turn the tile over. Maybe on the tile there's a quote from Bertrand Russell: "Boredom is a vital problem for the moralist since half the sins of mankind are caused by fear of it." You smile. No, just because boredom brings with it a whiff of the void, you aren't obliged to overdramatize the moment.

The second tile reads, "Boredom isn't an indictment of life." Boredom is just a bit of a meaning shortfall, a mini meaning crisis. As a student of meaning, you know that meaning comes and goes. That it has vanished for a bit is not so startling. You simply turn to your list of cherished life purposes (you've created that list, yes?) and decide where you want to make some meaning next. And, who knows, maybe this bit of boredom is a necessary precursor to some excellent creative activity. Turn the tile over. There's a lovely reminder from the artist Marianne Mathiasen: "I have noticed that after a day of boredom I get more creative, so perhaps our brain needs a rest from time to time." Hold boredom that way, rather than as a huge negative statement about life.

The third tile reads, "Boredom motivates me." You turn the tile over. There are two helpful quotes. From the sculptor Anish Kapoor: "It's precisely in those moments when I don't know what to do, boredom drives one to try a host of possibilities to either get somewhere or not get anywhere." From the artist Gustav Klimt: "Today I want to start working again in earnest—I'm looking forward to it because doing nothing does become rather boring after a while." You remember that working regularly and productively dispels boredom. You take this bit of boredom as an excellent reminder to return to your plan for your life.

The fourth tile reads, "What is this boredom masking?" Is it really boredom or is this fit of boredom masking some other feeling like resentment or rage? Read the two quotes on the underside of the tile. From the theologian Paul Tillich: "Boredom is rage spread thin." From the novelist G. K. Chesterton: "A yawn is a silent shout." If it isn't boredom, if it's something very different, get that challenge named. You know what to do next, don't you? Open the tactics drawer for *that* challenge, remove the tiles rattling around in there, and start battling the resentment or the rage.

The fifth tile reads, "Best me." This reminds you that you may not yet be the person you need to be in order to handle psychological challenges like boredom effectively. Indeed, maybe your formed personality habitually creates boredom, in which case you will want to employ your available personality to move in the direction of an improved you. Turn the tile over. Hear the philosopher Søren Kierkegaard: "Boredom is the root of all evil—the despairing refusal to be oneself." When you become your best self, boredom might just vanish as an issue.

You may want to create an actual tactics table and put together sets of tiles for dealing with the many challenges that we are obliged to handle in life. Whether or not you create an actual tactics table, make use of this metaphor when some unwanted state like boredom arrives. Say to yourself, "Off to the tactics table!" Feel like a great commander about to engage with a formidable enemy. Smile a little—and then go do battle.

Primary Issue: Boredom and Existential Sadness

- What other issues might this exercise help address?
- How might you personalize and customize this exercise?
- What are five thoughts that would align with and support this exercise's central intention?
- What five actions might you take so as to support any changes you consider important to make?

- How might you use your imagination and your native brilliance to customize this exercise, upgrade your personality, improve your experience of indwelling, or meet the challenge this exercise is addressing?
- Imagine that a quick, radical transformation in the direction suggested by this exercise might be possible. What might that transformation look like?

10 Dance, Smile, Scone

How shall we conceptualize the way the past informs and affects the present? Are past negative experiences, from tiny rebuffs and small slights to truly painful and traumatic events, residing somewhere in that room that is your mind, waiting to intrude and pounce? Are they like burrs on your easy chair, making that easy chair always prickly? Are they asleep and only awakened by some current experience that rouses them and that causes them to suddenly wail or to pinch? Where are they and why do they return?

The past certainly seems to return unbidden sometimes, completely disconnected from any current experience. There you are, walking along, thinking nothing in particular, and suddenly you're flooded with some terrible memory of the time that you made a huge mistake, the time that you were abused, or the time that you chose a path that proved rocky and led to nowhere. Why did that memory assault you just then? Were you thinking something out of conscious awareness that triggered the memory? Was it the look of the sky, a stray scent, or a passing scene? Can anyone say?

Let's suppose that sometimes that painful memory returning and flooding us is in fact the culmination of some just-out-of-conscious-awareness train of thought. Just how far out of conscious awareness was it? What if it was so very close that you could actually smell it, taste it, or sense it, if only you were alert to its presence? If that were true, if thought processes that lead to the return of painful memories can be sensed as they transpire—then couldn't they perhaps be interrupted and the memory avoided?

Think about how that interrupting might work. You're walking along. It's a sunny day. You suddenly sense just the slightest chill somewhere inside you. Plus, it's unnaturally quiet in there—too quiet for your own good. You can't tell what exactly you're thinking but you can feel that chill and hear that silence. You say, "Uh oh." You stop and do a little dance, maybe a bit of an Irish jig. You smile. You dance a bit more. You think about a scone with butter and jam. Which scone should it be? Are you in the mood for a currant and raisin scone? Would you prefer a savory one, maybe one with cheddar cheese and green onions? You smile. You dance a bit more. You proceed with your life—with no bad memory having attacked you.

Is there any way you can know for sure if you really spared yourself a painful memory? Can you be certain that the chill you felt and the silence you heard were warning signs of the past returning? No—how could you know? But what was the cost of that little insurance policy: nothing more than a smile or two, a little dancing, and some pleasant thoughts about a scone. Can that even be called a cost ... or was it more like a spontaneous one-minute vacation? Isn't that the perfect insurance policy, after all, one that is all joy and costs nothing?

Maybe you're a little worried about dancing down the street, smiling, and looking foolish. Let's hope not. You wouldn't want to pass on a simple, pleasant, and effective strategy because of some shyness. Really, couldn't you do with a little more street dancing, smiling, and scone dreaming? After all, there is the startling possibility that you might avoid some of your painful memories by sensing them coming and blocking their arrival just with a little dancing and smiling. You don't want to miss that chance, do you?

This may only be a slight possibility but it does conform to our experience. While these terrible memories seem to spring upon us unannounced, we nevertheless sensed that something was brewing, that the silence in our mind didn't sound quite right, that some whiff of ammonia got into our nostrils. Haven't you had that experience? So perhaps this will work beautifully to keep the past at bay.

Try it today. When you feel that something suspicious is going on in your mind, when you sense that some train of thought may be heading you toward a hurricane, start dancing, smiling, and contemplating scones. Or sing, laugh, and picture pancakes. The details are up to you. Whether it's dancing, smiling, and scones or singing, laughing, and pancakes, begin to pay attention to those silences and scents that signal the past returning and instantly start frolicking.

And if engaging in that helpful singing and dancing feels too embarrassing to do in public, do it in private, in the room that is your mind. No one will see you and you just might get the same excellent results!

Primary Issue: Dealing with the Return of Traumatic Memories

- What other issues might this exercise help address?
- How might you personalize and customize this exercise?
- What are five thoughts that would align with and support this exercise's central intention?
- What five actions might you take so as to support any changes you consider important to make?

- How might you use your imagination and your native brilliance to customize this exercise, upgrade your personality, improve your experience of indwelling, or meet the challenge this exercise is addressing?
- Imagine that a quick, radical transformation in the direction suggested by this exercise might be possible. What might that transformation look like?

11 Left Index Finger

We have the sense that thoughts reside in the mind, whose location seems to be in our head. But where do feelings reside? It would be nice if feelings had their own room, a room like the one that is our mind, so that we could do similar work on our feelings like the work we're doing on our mind. We might install windows in that room; we might get a second easy chair; and so on. That would be lovely and helpful. But we don't seem to experience feelings that way.

So, let's employ a different metaphor for feelings. Rather than imagining that they reside in a room, which doesn't feel true, let's imagine that they circulate in our system, the way that hot water or cool air circulates in our house. In fact, feelings seem to circulate like that, coursing through our bloodstream and our nervous system. Sometimes nothing is coursing through us; we feel rather neutral. If asked, we might say, "I'm not feeling anything in particular." But then something happens—a small incident on the bus, a toe stub, a bad memory, a desire—and we can almost hear that "Swoosh!" of a feeling suddenly circulating.

The anger. The sadness. The humiliation. The flooding of feeling that just about knocks us off our feet. And why shouldn't it affect us exactly that powerfully, if it's flowing everywhere in our system, through every pipe and into every nook and cranny? How it rushes everywhere, overwhelming thought and stealing the moment!

But isn't that image of a feeling coursing everywhere suggestive? What if you could isolate that coursing feeling a little bit? Think of a smart house with individual temperature zones, a house where you can make your bedroom toasty without having to heat the whole house. What if you could do that with feelings?

Imagine that you could isolate that bad feeling that just welled up in you, isolate it in, say, the index finger of your left hand. The feeling is coursing through you; you mentally send it in the direction of your hand; then you funnel it into your left index finger. Having done that excellent isolating, your finger is now the only place where you are feeling the feeling. Isn't that something?

Imagine what you could do at this point. You could use your index finger like a pistol and shoot that feeling at some imaginary target. You could use your finger like a graffiti pen and scrawl pungent graffiti on some imaginary wall. You could use your finger like an eyedropper and let the bile drip out into the sink. You could use your imagination to dream up all sorts of powerfully cleansing things to do with that now carefully contained and isolated feeling!

Probably you should start with a small emotion, maybe a bit of irritation. You've just missed your train. How frustrating! Stop. Breathe. Aim that feeling of irritation that's coursing through your system toward your left index finger. See how that works? After practicing that a few times, move on to a middle-sized emotion. You have a chat with one of your parents and get criticized. Okay. Here comes the emotion. Whoosh! It's everywhere, racing through your arteries and veins. Breathe. Yes, this is harder. But try. Aim that anguish and anger toward your left index finger. Maybe say something out loud like, "Get moving, you bad feeling!" Did it work? Maybe it did!

Now, let's try it out on a big emotion. We'll need to be very careful here. Big emotions are big. They can be horribly painful, maddeningly intense, even overwhelming. Breathe several times. Try to angle this big emotion toward your hand. This may prove much harder. But try. Now, corral it into your left index finger. That's a lot of emotion for one finger! But maybe you managed. Okay. Now ... get rid of it. Carefully squeeze it into the sink, using your left index finger like an eyedropper. Or use it as ink to paint like a Goya.

You will need more tactics than just this one to deal with your emotions. Spend a little time and dream up a few fanciful, provocative, potentially amazing strategies for dealing with the emotions that rise up in us every day. You don't want to do a wonderful job on your thoughts and let slide that other human endowment, your feelings. We've been working on dynamically self-regulating thoughts; but what about dynamically self-regulating feelings as well? Isn't that an excellent idea too?

Primary Issue: Dealing with Painful Feelings

- What other issues might this exercise help address?
- How might you personalize and customize this exercise?
- What are five thoughts that would align with and support this exercise's central intention?
- What five actions might you take so as to support any changes you consider important to make?
- How might you use your imagination and your native brilliance to customize this exercise, upgrade your personality, improve your experience of indwelling, or meet the challenge this exercise is addressing?
- Imagine that a quick, radical transformation in the direction suggested by this exercise might be possible. What might that transformation look like?

12 Sorting Through Injustices

People like you and me care about fairness. Injustice riles us, festers in us, and torments us. How unfair is that? Isn't it really unfair that, given how we'd prefer spending our time, maybe writing a spellbinding novel or tackling a scientific conundrum, we have to concern ourselves with the billion injustices perpetrated every day, from the tiny to the tragic? It would be one thing if we only cared about those injustices that directly affected us. But no, every single injustice that we learn about bothers us and provokes us.

Let's take one example of injustice. A tyrannical father beats his wife and his children mercilessly. This is intolerable to us; we enter the room that is our mind in a frenzy not knowing what to do with our rage and our incomprehension. We sit in our easy chair, which feels anything but easy, and play out a revenge fantasy; or we commit to redoubling our activism, knowing for certain that no amount of activism on our part will spare the next poor woman these men encounter; or we write a poem of anguish. Or, more usually, we sit there stewing until we do the following.

Most often what we do is pull open one of the drawers of the chest that is standing there in the corner of the room that is our mind, the drawer containing a thousand other injustices that we have collected over time and that we have no way of rectifying, and we stuff that new unbearable thought in there. Then we slam the drawer shut. We do this for our mental health, since we simply can't function if those thousand memories of monstrosities are allowed out to freely populate our mind.

Let's take a very different sort of injustice. Every month we get a certain bill and every month we are overcharged in the same cavalier, cynical way. It's only a few dollars; but still it's maddening. We know that the corporation sending us this bill is doing this on purpose, stealing these two or three dollars from millions of people. How amazingly irritating this theft feels! What can we realistically do? Stop their service and spend all that time finding another provider? Make an angry telephone call to an underpaid customer service representative? Inaugurate a class action suit? Heavens! No; eventually, after fifteen minutes or half an hour of stewing, we open that drawer and stuff this injustice away, thus adding to our storehouse of miserable memories.

Take a third sort of injustice. Your mate never really treated you fairly. But you put up with all that unfairness for all sorts of reasons. Now that you are divorced, you find yourself asking two insidious questions, "Why did I put up with that?" and "How can I get even?" Because the answer to the first may be, "I don't really want to know" and because the answer to the second quite likely is, "I really can't," you sit there stewing. Eventually those injustices go into the drawer kicking and screaming, becoming some of your worst memories.

We have stuffed into that drawer a really diverse and amazing collection of injustices. The way we were unjustly overcharged on a bill. Genocides. That rude, unfair thing a friend said about us. Corrupt politicians. That time our mate selfishly ate the last slice of pie. Killing fields. The objective size of the injustice has never been our criterion for holding onto it: if it feels like an injustice, we stuff it into that drawer, we add it to memory, and there it squirms, making wailing noises and too often crawling out to beleaguer us.

Is there a better way to handle these countless injustices? Well, you might try the following. Set aside a good portion of an afternoon. Enter the room that is your mind and pull up a stool in front of the chest of drawers where you've stuffed all those injustices. Take a deep breath and ask yourself the following question: "Would it serve me to open this drawer and sort through these injustices, maybe taking some large number of them to the trash? Or would that prove too overwhelming and risky?"

The answer may be that the task feels too daunting, in which case leave that room and go out in the sunshine. But it may be that you feel equal to the task and that you intuit that it would serve you to rid yourself of some of those thoughts and feelings. If so, get your sorting bags ready and make sure you're armed with twist ties. You will want to get those bags securely shut, as those injustices will be squirming! When you're done, shut the drawer tightly on whatever remains and celebrate that you've made a little room— because you'll need that room. You'll be adding to that drawer, don't you know, since more injustices are coming to confront and confound you!

Primary Issue: Challenges Connected with a Refined Sense of Fairness

- What other issues might this exercise help address?
- How might you personalize and customize this exercise?
- What are five thoughts that would align with and support this exercise's central intention?
- What five actions might you take so as to support any changes you consider important to make?
- How might you use your imagination and your native brilliance to customize this exercise, upgrade your personality, improve your experience of indwelling, or meet the challenge this exercise is addressing?
- Imagine that a quick, radical transformation in the direction suggested by this exercise might be possible. What might that transformation look like?

13 Mind Party

When was the last time you had a party in your mind? When was the last time you entered that room that is your mind with a bunch of balloons, put on some salsa music, and invited all those sad guests slumped here and there to get up and dance? When, that is, did you have some fun in your mind? Not very recently, I'm willing to bet!

We need more mind parties. Most days our mind is a workaday place, a gloomy place, a steam kettle, a piston-driven engine, and not a party venue. Wouldn't it be fun to decorate? And order a cake? And select a play list? And games! Lots of games! Not just another round of solitaire or a crossword puzzle or Sudoku puzzle but something lively, tumultuous, and over the top. Like, for instance, mind spin-the-bottle ...

Picture someone you loved to kiss. Get that champagne bottle out of the fridge, spin it, and where it points, there he or she is! Permission to kiss granted! Spin it again—oh, now it's *that* person. Excellent. Can you do too much kissing at the party in your mind? Not hardly!

Or try this mind party favorite. Invite everyone to tell a story. Select a theme: maybe a great childhood moment, a first travel adventure, or a strange starry night full of awe and wonder. Have the storytellers pass around a talking stick or maybe a talking pretzel. Let anyone pass who is too shy or entranced to speak. Thank each storyteller, and then bring out the cake!

Who will you invite? The lovely thing about a mind party is that no one will turn you down. Invite whomever you like and they will be there! Invite some couples who dance the tango. Invite a top expert in a field you'd love to learn. Invite a hero of yours. Invite an ancestor, maybe that one you've heard all those stories about, the one who stole horses or invented the cream puff. Invite you from different epochs and lives. Invite a whole mime troupe or maybe a performance artist who'll wrap your room in pink yarn. Mix and match to your heart's content! If anyone bores you or disappoints you, send him or her packing.

A fellow I know is writing a book about lightness. He believes that lightness will save us. We are all so heavy, he feels: we live so heavy, we communicate so heavy, we work so heavy, we even love heavy. Where is the lightness? Where are the marshmallows? Where are the giggles? Where are the summer afternoons? It appears that in order to have that lightness we must create it. It is perhaps a bit of irony and yet more unfortunate heaviness that in order to have lightness we must create it. But so be it. Dance time!

You may have some objections. Oh, a party in the mind is too silly. A party in the mind is too frivolous. A party in the mind is a pathetic self-indulgence. A party in the mind is just too goofy. What's the point? Well, a party in the mind isn't silly, frivolous, self-indulgent, goofy or pointless. It's a golden opportunity to lighten up, to smile, to get off the treadmill of mild sorrow that each of us is treading daily.

Of course, there's that most objectionable objection of all, that somehow you don't deserve it. As if because you've made some messes and tripped here and there you aren't entitled to joy. What an idea! Who sold you that bill of goods? Imagine a child saying to himself or herself, "I am too bad to deserve a birthday party." Doesn't that make you want to weep? Never think such a thing again. Parties in the mind are our eternal birthright!

What's the favorite party that I throw? It's a quote party where I invite my favorite quotes to visit. There's a Tchaikovsky quote about inspiration that I love, a Pavarotti quote about devotion, several Camus quotes (and whole passages), and, well, some of my own quotes, too, where I've turned a phrase that I'm happy to remember. I bring out the folding chairs, put up bunting, make cupcakes (quotes love cupcakes), and greet each quote at the door with a really heartfelt greeting, as they are very much cherished. What a lovely time we have!

Your mind needs more joy. Every mind does. A party may be just the ticket. Throw one soon and enjoy the festivities!

Primary Issue: Sadness and Despair

- What other issues might this exercise help address?
- How might you personalize and customize this exercise?
- What are five thoughts that would align with and support this exercise's central intention?
- What five actions might you take so as to support any changes you consider important to make?
- How might you use your imagination and your native brilliance to customize this exercise, upgrade your personality, improve your experience of indwelling, or meet the challenge this exercise is addressing?
- Imagine that a quick, radical transformation in the direction suggested by this exercise might be possible. What might that transformation look like?

14 Saying Goodnight

No sleep, no mental health.

Nothing is a better predictor that our mind is going to suffer than a lack of sleep. So many people are sleeping poorly or sleeping hardly at all nowadays. Why all this insomnia? Because folks are worrying around the clock; or, worse, tormenting themselves around the clock. This amounts to double trouble: first, all that persistent anxiety, and then the additional strain that sleeplessness produces.

Are you wide awake far too much of the time in that room that is your mind? When the moon is full, are you staring at it and not sleeping? When it's two in the morning, are you taking turns tossing, glancing at the clock, and pestering yourself with some thought? This is a grave problem. When your mind gets no chance to rest, when all that your mind has been doing, hour after hour in that eerie darkness, is stewing and bouncing thoughts from wall to wall, it starts to deteriorate, hallucinate, fabricate, and just plain sicken. Your mind needs its rest!

How can you get it some rest? You might count sheep. You might take some chemical, which might produce the effect you want, but which likely will come accompanied by profound negative side effects. One well-known actor pictured a red dot that he made larger and smaller and larger and smaller until he wore himself out. Maybe you have your own favorite tricks. Maybe it has to do with how you prop your pillows. Maybe it has to do with some special tea. Everyone is trying something because everyone is having trouble sleeping, living in a fog, and on the brink of decomposing.

What else might you try? Here's one possibility. Ceremonially say goodnight to everything in the room that is your mind as if you were saying goodnight to all those beloved stuffed animals with which you populated your childhood bedroom. Visit the room that is your mind and say goodnight to the concert poster. "Good night, concert poster!" Say goodnight to the pile of unpaid bills. "Good night, bills!" Say goodnight to the slight you experienced at work. "Good night, slight!" Say goodnight to the memory that keeps haunting you. "Good night, memory!" Say a gentle, pleasant goodnight to each and every thing, to the objects, the worries, the dust mites, and the laundry.

Say goodnight to the windows you installed, to your safety valve, to your easy chair, to all the fittings you've provided yourself to make your mind the most hospitable place you can make it. And say some special goodnights. Do you have a grandchild halfway across the globe who makes you smile when you think of her but who also brings you pain because you see her so rarely? Wish her a special goodnight. Say, "I love you, granddaughter. I wish I could see you more! But here I am hugging you, dearest. Goodnight, love."

Do you have a pestering thought that has pestered you for eternity, maybe the thought that you just aren't talented enough to write your novel or attractive enough to compete in the singles' world? Say a special goodnight to that thought. That special goodnight might sound something like the following: "Enough about talent, mind. I love the idea for my novel. Let me just try to write it. Peace to you, unfortunate thought. Goodnight to you, unfortunate thought. Sleep very tight!"

As you quiet yourself for sleep, be gentle, peaceful, and comforting in that room that is your mind. Be gentle with each object, each worry, and each memory. Be as peaceful as you can be. Sing a lullaby to the umbrella stand. Pat the desktop. Unfold your patchwork comforter. Listen for the sounds of sleep around you, the light snoring of vague and distant memories, the rhythmic breathing of your kindness toward yourself, the whispers of dreams arriving. Be gentle, quiet, and comforting as you tiptoe about shutting down your mind for the night.

Your electronic devices have a way of powering down even if you forget to shut them off. They go to sleep and that conserves them. Your way of conserving yourself is exactly the same: a good night's sleep. If that good night's sleep eludes you too often, your mind will begin to wear down. You may become strange to yourself, edgy, paranoid, unlikeable, and miserable. Your mind really does need its rest. Tonight, if the moon is too bright and your thoughts are too pestering, try making the rounds of your mind and saying a sweet goodnight to anyone and anything still awake in there.

Primary Issue: Insomnia and Sleep Deprivation Issues

- What other issues might this exercise help address?
- How might you personalize and customize this exercise?
- What are five thoughts that would align with and support this exercise's central intention?
- What five actions might you take so as to support any changes you consider important to make?
- How might you use your imagination and your native brilliance to customize this exercise, upgrade your personality, improve

your experience of indwelling, or meet the challenge this exercise is addressing?

- Imagine that a quick, radical transformation in the direction suggested by this exercise might be possible. What might that transformation look like?

15 Hot Lava, Ice Water

The inside of the earth is boiling hot and produces lava. The inside of a human being is boiling wild and produces terrible impulses and even the occasional monster. We call all that boiling wildness our primitive nature and suppose that it arises from some ancient, less refined part of our brain, some place of lizards and violent solutions. But who can say? Maybe it came just from yesterday or even from today. Are we really so civilized?

How does this roiling manifest itself? You may be thinking a very ordinary thought like, "Do I want butter or cream cheese with my bagel?" and right under that thought a sea of a hot lava is roiling, ready to cascade out as a terrible episode of binge drinking, a truly careless affair that sends your whole life reeling, a horrible remark that you can never take back, or a violent gesture that no apology will ever make right. Strange to say, it may even manifest as a slovenly day of pajamas, fig bars, and television. To contain our hot lava sometimes we become a couch potato. How odd we are!

That lava is boiling in each of us, fiery red and as hot as hell, which makes our mind a house built on a volcano. Each of us lives in that danger zone. Can't you sense all that hot lava roiling even as you try to decide between butter and cream cheese for your bagel? I think you can. I think you can sense its presence through the cracks and the fissures of consciousness as it sizzles away down there, ready to erupt. And that you can sense it is a great thing. That means that you can prepare for those eruptions.

How? By keeping a bucket of ice water handy. Picture the room that is your mind. Identify the spot where you'll locate your bucket of ice water. Will you put it directly beneath that favorite painting of yours (maybe the one of apricots, from a forthcoming exercise)? Or just to the left of the umbrella stand? Now picture those glints of lava peeking through the floor. Something wild is about to be wanted of you. Your insides are about to demand that you drop everything and rush off at two hundred miles an hour, screeching down the street like a wild person. What to do?

Calmly retrieve your bucket of ice water, prepare yourself for that fiery arrival of lava, and when those first threads of molten lava seep up, douse them with the ice water. What a steam bath you'll create! You'll have trouble seeing and trouble breathing. You may well be obliged to cough for a full minute. But you will have doused out that hot lava for the moment, maybe even for a day or a month. And maybe you'll even turn that hot lava into solid lava rock, sealing up the fissures and making the ground more solid beneath your feet. Isn't that where Hawaii came from? And isn't that a lovely thought, that maybe you can transform your boiling insides into a tropical paradise just by having a bucket of ice water handy?

Even if you don't produce paradise, you will have prevented an escapade that might cost you your marriage, your liver, or your self-respect, cooled down your desire for revenge to an ember, made way for a reconciliation that is much to be preferred to hatred, or done something else good for your system. Yes, you had to tolerate some steam. Yes, that red glow was beautiful. Yes, you may actually prefer fire to ice. But the cost of letting that lava come flowing in is terrible self-scorching.

Do the following right now. Situate a bucket of ice water in your mind. You can keep it off in a corner, if you like, but don't hide it behind that huge stuffed tiger or that pile of unread books. You want to be able to see it and you want to know that it is there. Yes, a fire extinguisher doesn't add much to a room's décor and likewise your water bucket won't prettify your mind. But the goal isn't elegance. The goals are safety and self-respect. We do not respect ourselves if we let hot lava rule. We can explain our behavior to ourselves after the fact—I had a terrible impulse, I couldn't control myself!— but that's a little late, isn't it? Wouldn't it have been much better to douse that impulse when it was just a red glow peeking through the floor?

Primary Issue: Mania and other Racing Brain Challenges

- What other issues might this exercise help address?
- How might you personalize and customize this exercise?
- What are five thoughts that would align with and support this exercise's central intention?
- What five actions might you take so as to support any changes you consider important to make?
- How might you use your imagination and your native brilliance to customize this exercise, upgrade your personality, improve your experience of indwelling, or meet the challenge this exercise is addressing?
- Imagine that a quick, radical transformation in the direction suggested by this exercise might be possible. What might that transformation look like?

16 The One-Word Solution

In a well-known German novel, *Billiards at Half-Past Nine* by Heinrich Böll, a character has the same lunch every day: cottage cheese sprinkled with paprika. He is not a very likeable character. He is stiff, unbending, and ultimately cruel. Then there was someone I knew who brought the same supposedly healthy lunch to work every day for years—a tuna fish sandwich—and became demented from all that mercury. Repeating ourselves is fine, but a too-steady diet of the same thing can signal that we are living a small and straightjacketed life. Repetition can prove risky—and it's the same with our thoughts.

Say that you're thinking a thought that doesn't serve you. Thinking it once is unfortunate. But thinking it a million times, hour after hour and day after day, hijacks your life. Just imagine thinking, "I have no chance" over and over again. Imagine it blinking in green neon opposite your easy chair in the room that is your mind. How easy would that easy chair feel if you had to look at that malignant indictment every second? All day and all night: "I have no chance." You take a nap and you wake up and there it is again: "I have no chance." How would a life lived in that way feel?

There are serious things to do to try to stop caustic repetitions of that sort. But there are also amusing and goofy things to try. Here is an amusing and goofy one. Simply change one word of the thought. Put in any new word you like. Instead of thinking, "I have no chance," think "I have no socks" or "I have no celery" or "Goats have no chance." Silly, isn't it? But who's to say that silly can't also be brilliant?

Maybe the repetitive thought is "Nothing about life is fair." Change one word. "Nothing about paragliding is fair" or "Nothing about life is purple." Maybe the repetitive thought is "There's so much competition." Change one word. "There's so much shortcake" or "There's so much alfalfa." Does changing a word in this fashion make life fair or reduce the competition you face? No, it doesn't. But it may disrupt your pattern of self-talk, momentarily end the trance you're in, and allow you to laugh just a little. Isn't that something?

We know all about repetitive, unproductive, obsessive self-talk. We know how debilitating and damaging that self-talk can be. If we ask ourselves again and again, "Did I lock the door?" we wear ourselves out and kidnap neurons that might otherwise be used for good work. Isn't that the essence of mental staleness, boredom, and agitation? "Oh, my gosh, not that thought again!" How tiring! How maddening! But there it is. Given this terrible penchant for repeating ourselves, we need as many tactics as we can muster in order to interrupt that onslaught.

These are exactly the sorts of tactics and strategies that cognitive therapists regularly offer, tactics like thought stopping and thought substituting. But rarely are their tactics amusing or absurd-seeming. They are professionals, after all, these cognitive therapists, with a professional demeanor to uphold. It wouldn't do for them to present you with a silly strategy. But silly might be just what the doctor ordered. Imagine saying "I have no flies" rather than "I have no chance"? Don't you feel better already?

You could of course change a word because you want to make a point to yourself, for example by changing "I have no chance" to "I have some chance" or by changing "Nothing about life is fair" to "Lots about life is fair." We would understand your intention in each instance: you are wanting to paint a picture of life as better. That makes perfect sense. But for my little exercise I would like you to be sillier than that and head in the direction of nonsense. Pick words that make no contextual sense and create sentences that are patently ridiculous. I am trying to get you to smile! Please play along and see what you experience.

Get yourself ready. When you think a thought that you know doesn't serve you, say to yourself, "If I have that thought again today, I'm changing one word and turning it goofy." If that thought arrives a second time, smile, say it out loud—for instance, "I have no chance"—and then say it again with a word substituted. "I have no raisins." "I have no walnuts." This may not get to the heart of the matter but it may make you giggle and provide you with a respite; and giggling and respites are not nothing.

Primary Issue: Repetitive, Unproductive, Obsessive Thinking

- What other issues might this exercise help address?
- How might you personalize and customize this exercise?
- What are five thoughts that would align with and support this exercise's central intention?
- What five actions might you take so as to support any changes you consider important to make?
- How might you use your imagination and your native brilliance to customize this exercise, upgrade your personality, improve your experience of indwelling, or meet the challenge this exercise is addressing?
- Imagine that a quick, radical transformation in the direction suggested by this exercise might be possible. What might that transformation look like?

17 River Path

How you evaluate life matters since you experience life against the backdrop of your evaluation of life. If your evaluation of life is negative, nothing has much of a chance of feeling positive. What if you've gone so far as to evaluate life as a complete cheat? Isn't that evaluation bound to promote chronic sadness? Very likely it is.

Why might you have evaluated life that harshly? Maybe it's because you went unloved as a child. Maybe it's because you have to spend a stupendous amount of your time just earning a living. Maybe it's because you never met your soul mate. Maybe it's because you see immorality rewarded and good deeds punished.

Maybe it's because you had dreams that never materialized and goals that you never met. Maybe it's because you see clearly how money is unfairly distributed. Maybe it's because you just expected *more* out of life—more from it, more from others, more from yourself. Indeed, it may be easier and more natural to evaluate life as a cheat than to evaluate it as something worth the candle. In its own way, that seems completely reasonable.

A great many people have evaluated life as a cheat without, however, realizing that they have made this decision and without realizing how many unfortunate consequences flow from this decision. Still, even though you may have ample reasons to feel that life is a cheat, you must evaluate life as worth living. You must decide that life matters. Can you manage to evaluate life in a positive way even though you've been badly disappointed in the past and even though you find life taxing and unrewarding? That is a conversation that you must have with yourself.

Do have this conversation, as hard as it may prove. Visit the room that is your mind, settle yourself into your easy chair, enjoy the warmth of the fire blazing in the fireplace opposite, and ask yourself the hard question, "Could it be that I've evaluated life as a cheat?" If the answer is yes or maybe, ask the follow-up question: "What can I do to change my mind and give life a thumb's up, even if it doesn't quite deserve it?" Please ask and try to answer these questions.

Maybe your easy chair isn't quite the place for this conversation. If it turns out not to be, let's design a special place in the room that is your mind for these important, difficult existential conversations. Maybe you'd be better off having this conversation while taking a stroll. In that case, let's add a shady path by the river to the room that is your mind. Saunter by the river, enjoy a lovely summer's day, and chat with yourself about how exactly you're going to go about giving life a thumb's up.

Because we human beings wall off knowledge that upsets us, we may well not know that we have evaluated life as pointless, a cheat, and a fraud. It might be expected that we would get some clues from our behaviors—that we drink a lot, that we take antidepressants, that we fantasize about taking our revenge—but we may find it just too painful to announce the cause of our suffering, that we have evaluated life negatively. A great many people, maybe even the vast majority, have come to negative conclusions and evaluations about life but deny that they have given life a thumb's down.

If you agree that how you evaluate life colors how you perceive your experiences, provides you or fails to provide you with motivational juice, and largely determines whether or not you will bother to live according to your principles, you must attempt the odd work of thoughtfully deciding if you can possibly evaluate life more positively. Maybe, just maybe, you can find the way to do that. Maybe, that is, you can come down on the side of affirming that life matters.

If you paint this different sort of picture for yourself, one that conceptualizes life not as a cheat and a fraud but as a project, an obligation, an opportunity to make yourself proud, and even as an adventure, you will discover that you experience meaning more often and that those experiences of meaning begin to accumulate and count. Meaninglessness may even begin to recede as an issue. Go the room that is your mind right now and have this conversation. Maybe you'll have it sitting in your easy chair, maybe a walk by the river will suit you better, whatever way you decide to design your experience, it's time to deal with the possibility that your negative evaluation of life may be dragging you down.

Primary Issue: Evaluating Life as a Cheat

- What other issues might this exercise help address?
- How might you personalize and customize this exercise?
- What are five thoughts that would align with and support this exercise's central intention?
- What five actions might you take so as to support any changes you consider important to make?
- How might you use your imagination and your native brilliance to customize this exercise, upgrade your personality, improve your experience of indwelling, or meet the challenge this exercise is addressing?
- Imagine that a quick, radical transformation in the direction suggested by this exercise might be possible. What might that transformation look like?

18 Bedrock

So as to deal with meaning earthquakes (that is, meaning crises that shake your very foundation), let's build the room that is your mind on solid bedrock. To begin, let's get a little clear on the nature of meaning. Meaning is a private, personal, individual, and subjective psychological experience. Every argument for the objectivity of meaning is merely the attempt by someone to elevate his subjective experience and his opinions above yours and mine. Meaning is personal and subjective.

Whether you find it more meaningful to sit for an hour by a pond watching ducks paddle or more meaningful to hop up after two minutes and rush home to work on your screenplay is entirely your decision—and one that you might change tomorrow. Because this is what meaning actually is—a certain sort of subjective psychological experience—it naturally follows that it will come and go. You may be experiencing something as meaningful—your career, the lecture you're attending, the book you're reading—and then suddenly you don't. Meaning can and does drain away, leak out, lapse, and otherwise vanish. That happens all the time.

The only way that you can create settled meaning is by giving away your freedom. You could end your meaning challenges with a lobotomy or by allowing others to tell you what to value, but those aren't very attractive options. Your better option is to forthrightly accept, even though you might want it to be otherwise, that your meanings are bound to shift and that your experience of life will vary from the very meaningful to the full-out meaningless.

Consider the following example. On Monday, you make a pledge to yourself to get fit and to take care of your body. On Tuesday, getting some devastating news about your son's health, you offer up one of your organs to save his life, putting your own body at risk. On Wednesday (some months later, having recovered from your operation), hearing troubling news about a threat to your country, you support your son's decision to enlist, even though enlisting constitutes a threat to his life, the life you recently gave one of your organs to save. On Thursday (of the following month), having learned more about the war in question, you protest your country's involvement and you fervently wish that your child could come back from that war—right now. These are the sorts of earthquakes in meaning that each of us may experience.

Or take the following example. You wake up one Saturday morning enthusiastic to buy a filing cabinet so that you can organize the notes for the novel that you are writing. You drive to the mall, energized because this little expedition is in the service of your meaning-making needs. At the mall, you start to sink a little. You recognize that not a soul you are passing is a member of the audience for your novel. The thought begins to percolate that you are wasting your time writing a novel that precious few people will read.

You find the right filing cabinet; but you already don't care. It is considerably more expensive than you had intended to pay but if you don't buy it, your day will feel even more meaningless, so you buy it, and now you are awash with a pair of bad feelings, that you just spent an extravagant amount of money on a filing cabinet for a book that no one will want and also that you should have gone to law school or taken over the family business, which, though boring, serves people's needs. By the time you get home from the mall with your filing cabinet, filing is the next to last thing on your mind (writing your novel is the last thing). Pouring a very tall Scotch is the first.

These earthquakes are bound to occur. What can help is imagining that the foundation under the room that is your mind is built on bedrock. You deal with every life purpose question, identity issue, and meaning shift from the solid footing of a deep understanding that these challenges are a part of life. You counteract the experience of existential vacuum and any whiffs of meaninglessness by visiting the room that is your mind and feeling how solid the floor feels under your feet. Braced by this solid foundation, you announce, "I can survive this earthquake."

You may still be shaking but the ground beneath you isn't. You murmur, "I'm sure that meaning will return." You smile a little at how well you've built the room that is your mind, erecting it not on landfill or marshland but on ancient, indomitable bedrock. Yes, meaning is a problem—it is for all smart, sensitive, creative people—but you have the answer: that while you're actively making new meaning investments and seizing new meaning opportunities, the ground beneath you will remain as solid as a rock.

Primary Issue: Meaninglessness and Other Meaning Challenges

- What other issues might this exercise help address?
- How might you personalize and customize this exercise?
- What are five thoughts that would align with and support this exercise's central intention?
- What five actions might you take so as to support any changes you consider important to make?

- How might you use your imagination and your native brilliance to customize this exercise, upgrade your personality, improve your experience of indwelling, or meet the challenge this exercise is addressing?
- Imagine that a quick, radical transformation in the direction suggested by this exercise might be possible. What might that transformation look like?

19 Rebound Corner

Our feelings get hurt, often on a daily basis. We may pride ourselves on our rationality but how can we think clearly if our feelings are hurting? Rather often we can only think a useful thought *after* a painful feeling has subsided. The feeling may be too powerful for us to think clearly right in the split second of feeling that feeling. However, when that feeling *has* subsided, then it is our job to decide what we want to think.

Mary, a painter, sent her slides off to a gallery where she had high hopes for representation. What she got back was the terse email, "You are such an amateur!" Mary stopped painting for the next three years. Such dramatically unfortunate events happen all too often in the lives of creatives. One sharp criticism can derail an artist not only for far too long but sometimes altogether, making him completely doubt that he has the right or the wherewithal to be a professional artist—or any artist at all.

The consequences of receiving a blow of this sort are so severe primarily because of our powerful initial reaction to them, one that is often *so outsized and huge*. When someone says, either in veiled language or in no uncertain terms, that you are an idiot, that you have no talent, that you're a fool, that you're mediocre, that you're a hack, that you're derivative, that you're ... fill in the blank ... you *will* have a reaction. Often it is a whole-body, hard-to-tolerate emotional reaction that shifts your world, your world view, and your identity.

Virtually everyone has exactly such strong, visceral reactions to being criticized, humiliated or shamed. These powerful, automatic whole-body reactions, like our blushing response or our fight-or-flight response, are fundamental, hard-wired parts of who we are. Maybe some very advanced human being can avoid feeling these things; maybe some very detached human being can avoid feeling these things. For the rest of us, we *will* feel them. It will feel as if a tremendously large, bad event has happened—and yet all that has *really* happened is that we are having a feeling.

Once we have that feeling, then the ball is in our court. What are we going to do *next*? What you do next may affect how you spend the next year or even the rest of your life. If you take this pain and this criticism in without doing anything to defuse them or dispute them, you may lose a great deal of time or, even if you manage to continue creating, work much less strongly than you otherwise might. Much better is the following.

Create a corner in the room that is your mind, a rebound corner, where you go immediately when a powerful negative feeling strikes. When you get there, acknowledge that something has happened. Recognize that you suddenly find yourself awash in stress chemicals, negative thoughts, and bad feelings. Second, even as you admit that something has happened, reject that anything *really important* has happened. Alert yourself to the fact that you are just feeling a feeling. You may only be able to do this after the initial pain has subsided but after the first few seconds or few minutes of being blindsided you may be able to make this announcement. Third, say "Sooner rather than later." This is your rebound mantra and signifies your intention to get over this feeling sooner rather than later.

Once the pain has subsided, you can leave your rebound corner, settle yourself in your easy chair, and engage in a courageous assessment of the situation. It is hard to engage in that truthful assessment until you've simmered down a bit but once you've simmered down, you can do exactly that. Maybe a visitor comes into your studio and says, "Wow, these paintings are pretty dead!"

After you've calmed yourself and healed yourself in your rebound corner, you may be able to come to your own true assessment of the situation. That assessment might be, "Ridiculous!" Or that assessment might be, "Yes, I see how trying to 'copy' my really alive photographic collages onto the canvas has produced fairly dead paintings. I've known that for a while. Okay, now I fully accept that truth. I can't do that any longer." Once you've dealt with the painful criticism, you can decide what you want to make of the accusation.

These blows come regularly. When they do, we are suddenly awash in feelings. A key to emotional health is training ourselves how to get over these feelings sooner rather than later. We don't want to try to instantly stuff those feelings away in an old shoe box, as efforts of that sort have their own negative consequences. But we do want to move on from them as quickly as we can. Create a rebound corner in the room that is your mind where you know to go to feel painful feelings, acknowledge their pain, and release them as fast as possible.

Primary Issue: Dealing with Painful Feelings

- What other issues might this exercise help address?
- How might you personalize and customize this exercise?
- What are five thoughts that would align with and support this exercise's central intention?
- What five actions might you take so as to support any changes you consider important to make?

- How might you use your imagination and your native brilliance to customize this exercise, upgrade your personality, improve your experience of indwelling, or meet the challenge this exercise is addressing?
- Imagine that a quick, radical transformation in the direction suggested by this exercise might be possible. What might that transformation look like?

20 Winter Overcoat

It can prove a seriously heavy burden to need life to feel meaningful: that is, to have the experience of writing your novel or running your lab experiment feel meaningful as you are writing it or running it. That need can feel as burdensome as wearing your heaviest winter overcoat at the height of summer.

On top of the actual work required to live the project that is our life, must we add to that burden by needing our efforts to feel meaningful? Wouldn't just living our life-purpose choices prove arduous enough? But no—we look to be built to need to burden life with the demand that it must feel meaningful in the living.

What to do to deal with this unfortunate penchant? Get much more relaxed in the territory of meaning. Remove that winter overcoat! Do not demand of experiences that they feel meaningful. Live your life-purpose choices in your shirtsleeves! Indeed, as soon as you burden an experience with the need that it must feel meaningful, you're likely to have reduced its ability to provide that psychological experience. Do not burden experiences that way!

Let's say that you begin writing a novel because it wells up in you to write that novel. At that split second of beginning, you're not thinking about whether or not writing it is going to prove meaningful—you just want to start writing it. *That* unburdened experience is likely to provide you with the psychological experience of meaning. You needed nothing from the experience of writing it; you only wanted to write it; and as a result, writing it is likely to prove meaningful.

However, say that you are hungry for meaning and you make the conscious decision that writing a novel will constitute one of your meaning-making activities and that you expect that working on it will provide you with the psychological experience of meaning. In this instance—and ironically enough—you may find yourself less likely to experience meaning. A self-conscious demand on an activity that it *should feel meaningful* is likely to reduce its chances of actually feeling meaningful.

Of course, you want life to feel meaningful. At the same time, you do not want to burden your efforts with the demand that they feel meaningful. You can cherish the *hope* that something will provide you with the experience of joy without attaching to it the *need* that it provides you with that experience. As an analogy, you can hope that the vacation you are about to take will prove enjoyable, maybe by virtue of all of the sunbathing you intend to do, without *needing* the vacation to prove enjoyable. Then if it happens to rain every day while you are there, you may still be able to enjoy the vacation, because you weren't attached to all that sunbathing. Likewise, you can *hope* that a given meaning opportunity produces the experience of meaning without attaching to *needing* it to produce that experience.

You can't force life to mean and you don't want to try to force life to mean. Rather, you want to make conscious decisions about what efforts you think amount to value-based meaning-making efforts that support your life purpose choices—and then you want to *relax*. This deep relaxation is a philosophical stance that translates as: "I choose to do this next thing because I see it as a thing of value; and who knows what will happen." To support this wise stance, visit the room that is your mind, go to the closet you've installed there (you'll use this closet for other purposes as well), remove that burdensome winter overcoat, and hang it up on a sturdy hanger. Good riddance to it!

This is what "making meaning" entails: you value, you choose, you do, and then whatever happens, happens. As a result, you experience a sense of pride at having chosen, valued, and done something, even if you don't happen to experience meaning from the activity itself. And if you do experience meaning, that's something to celebrate! You point yourself in the direction of meaning, make the requisite effort, and then relax.

If life feels heavy, notice what you're wearing. Is it that heavy winter overcoat? If it is, you now know what to do. You go directly to the room that is your mind and, as you would upon entering any warm, indoor dwelling, you remove your overcoat and hang it up. This is the lightness of being that you're after! You can have it as easily as removing your coat.

Primary Issue: Requiring that Experiences Feel Meaningful

- What other issues might this exercise help address?
- How might you personalize and customize this exercise?
- What are five thoughts that would align with and support this exercise's central intention?
- What five actions might you take so as to support any changes you consider important to make?
- How might you use your imagination and your native brilliance to customize this exercise, upgrade your personality, improve

your experience of indwelling, or meet the challenge this exercise is addressing?

- Imagine that a quick, radical transformation in the direction suggested by this exercise might be possible. What might that transformation look like?

21 Old Friend

All of the thinking that we do, from calculating to problem-solving to predicting, produces a certain amount of anxiety. This natural anxiety might be handled relatively easily if we just remembered that it was coming and if we possessed some anxiety-management techniques to deal with it. Our usual way, however, is to not see the anxiety coming, to have no good plan in place for dealing with it, to be surprised anew each time it arrives, and, instead of handling the anxiety well, employing one of the following unfortunate anxiety reduction methods.

Maybe we flee the encounter—that is, we run away from the activity of thinking. We begin to think and almost immediately we get up and do something else; or we stay put but send our mind, we stay put but choose a different, easier problem to solve

Or maybe we employ dangerous "canalizing" tactics so as to make ourselves stay put: we scratch at our head, maybe until it bleeds, we bite our fingernails, maybe until they're bitten down, we keep a Scotch bottle or a pack of cigarettes handy, or in some other unhelpful way soothe ourselves as we struggle to think.

Or maybe we think small. Maybe we have a certain novel in mind to write. We sit down to begin it, anxiety quickly wells up in us, and we decide to write a blog post instead. Writing that blog post allows us to congratulate ourselves on having gotten *something* done—but inevitably those congratulations turn to chagrin, since we know exactly what our real intention was when we sat down.

Or maybe we play it safe in other ways. It is much easier on the brain for it to be asked to repeat a memorized message than to think. Most people who regularly communicate with others do not think on their feet, as that is hard, anxiety-provoking work. Instead, they craft a message and then repeat it. Those repeated messages are woven into their stump speech or become the tapes that they run. We sound more intelligent and more confident and do a better job of staying on point when we just repeat our messages. But where's the creativity, innovation, or heart in that?

Or maybe we begin to fantasize. As soon as that thinking anxiety begins to mount, a smart person, someone who naturally loves story, metaphor, narrative, and fantasy, can easily stop working on his novel and instead fantasize about winning the Nobel Prize. He lets his mind wander and fantasizes success, conquests, revenge, or anything else that might prove soothing and distracting. Because the brain of a smart person is so agile, it can spin itself lovely fantasies all day long, winning a battle with ferocious creatures in the morning, winning at love at midday, and winning a Pulitzer in the evening. But fantasizing doesn't get diseases cured or novels written.

Or maybe we over-prepare ourselves by doing a little more researching or leaving our work to read another book or attend another lecture. In a corner of awareness, we likely know exactly the game we're playing—which further distresses us, disappoints us, and raises our anxiety level.

Or maybe we try to circumvent the process. We might well wish that the process was different and, if we do wish that, we may find ourselves attracted to seminars on "the ten tricks for mistake-free thinking" or "the secret to perfect thinking." But what we are actually doing is avoiding the process, avoiding the anxiety, and avoiding doing the thinking.

John, a medical researcher, explained to me:

> I use all these methods! I had no idea that my cigarette smoking, my procrastinating, my fantasizing, my reading yet another journal article, my opting for a tiny corner of my field, are all connected at this base level, as ways to avoid the anxiety of thinking. Now I see exactly how they connect! I have to face the fact that aiming my brain at a difficult research question and tackling that question is going to make me anxious—period. I have to embrace that truth … and deal with it!

What ought you to do instead? Greet the anxiety and embrace it as an old friend. Yes, you'd prefer that he not visit; yes, he isn't really a friend, but he isn't a stranger, either, or an enemy. He's a feature of our early warning system alerting us to danger and in that regard, he is surely not our enemy. Greet him—and manage him effectively. There are scores of techniques to try—breathing techniques, cognitive techniques, relaxation techniques, stress-discharge techniques, reorienting techniques, disidentification techniques, and many more. Learn what to do when anxiety visits.

There you are, sitting in your easy chair in the room that is your mind, thinking hard about something. You notice that some anxiety is welling up. This no longer surprises you—now you know better than to be surprised. You murmur, "Hello, old friend, let me get out my snow globe and calm myself." You smile a little. You rather expected his visit. You know that he can't be barred from the room that is your mind and you've learned—or are learning—how to make his visit as short as possible.

Primary Issue: Effectively Managing the Anxiety of Thinking

- What other issues might this exercise help address?
- How might you personalize and customize this exercise?
- What are five thoughts that would align with and support this exercise's central intention?
- What five actions might you take so as to support any changes you consider important to make?
- How might you use your imagination and your native brilliance to customize this exercise, upgrade your personality, improve your experience of indwelling, or meet the challenge this exercise is addressing?
- Imagine that a quick, radical transformation in the direction suggested by this exercise might be possible. What might that transformation look like?

22 The Complete Answer

You're sitting in your easy chair in front of your blazing fire. You are trying to solve a problem. You give it some thought, then you shake your head. Too hard! You give up. The problem remains. That wasn't very successful, was it? But what if you had a method for getting solutions to the problems you posed yourself? Wouldn't that be something?

Here is one such method, an eight-step method. If you can begin to turn this method into a habit, you can start to get complete answers to the questions you pose yourself. First, you identify an issue—what exactly is the problem? Second, you examine its significance. Third, you identify the core questions that need answering. Fourth, you tease out your real intentions. Fifth, you notice what personality shadows get activated as you wrestle with this issue. Sixth, you identify the strengths you bring to the table. Seventh, you align your thoughts with any new intentions you've formed. Eighth, you align your behaviors with those new intentions. That's it!

How might this process work? Imagine a painter who is having trouble making sense of the next steps in her art career. She paints pretty regularly, is pretty happy with both the number of paintings she finishes and with their quality, but feels stuck trying to decide "how to market herself." She can't really align her thoughts with her intentions yet because she doesn't have any *clear* intentions, just the general intention "to market myself somehow." Her new thinking might proceed as follows:

> Okay, I know I need to market myself. This isn't just a "should" from somebody else's agenda but something that matters to me and that I have to own as important. I can't just pile up finished canvases from now until the end of time and feel good about myself as a painter. So, what exactly am I supposed to do? My head swims just thinking about it! There's so much advice out there—and so few painters making it! I think that the people selling the advice are the only ones making money! But ... I know that successful painters do exist. Maybe they're

the exceptions that prove the rule, but those exceptions do exist. So, let me stay positive!

I think the central question I need to address is, am I imagining that I'm going the gallery route or am I taking some other route? If I go the gallery route, what is the smartest way to proceed? If I mean to take some other route, what *are* those other routes? Well, I can try to make my studio my gallery, invite prospective buyers here, and try to do it all myself. I can create a website—but will that amount to anything but a very pretty business card seen by no one? If I don't get *publicity* and if I don't make a *name* for myself, what good is a pretty website or a studio that doubles as a gallery? So—doesn't it make sense to focus on "getting a name"? But what does *that* mean?

Okay. My intention is to figure out how an unknown painter acquires a name for herself. Well, that brings up all sorts of issues. I'm not really prepared to stand out or make waves—I see myself as an introvert who prefers the studio and doesn't do all that well in the world. How can "that sort of person" make a name for herself? And I'm usually an advice-taker and would customarily turn to a book, a website or a workshop to get this information. But mustn't this understanding of how to make a name for myself come from me for it to fit me and seem real?

I'm not sure exactly how to proceed but I do feel that I have an intention: to figure out how to make a name for myself as a painter. And I think that I have the basic smarts, ambition, energy, and backbone to pull that off. So, in order to keep my thoughts aligned with that intention, I am going to begin to say the following things to myself. I am going to say, "I can prove the exception." I am going to say, "I can figure out how to make a name for myself." When I hear myself saying things like "You have no chance," I am going to counter that thought with, "You don't serve me, thought!"

As to aligning my behaviors with my intention, first of all I'm going to do some basic research on strategies for "making a name for yourself." A lot of those strategies I want to rule out quickly if they sound too run-of-the-mill. But if I find one or two that have a feeling of rightness to them, I will start on them immediately. After I've done that basic research I'll check back in with myself to make sure that I am holding the right intention, and if I feel that I am then I'll get cracking and put into practice whatever I've learned.

The next time you encounter a problem—personal, professional, or creative—say to yourself, "I think I can arrive at the complete answer if I just sit here calmly and proceed systematically." Your comfy easy chair is waiting for you. And now you have a method!

Primary Issue: Ineffective Problem-Solving

- What other issues might this exercise help address?
- How might you personalize and customize this exercise?
- What are five thoughts that would align with and support this exercise's central intention?
- What five actions might you take so as to support any changes you consider important to make?
- How might you use your imagination and your native brilliance to customize this exercise, upgrade your personality, improve your experience of indwelling, or meet the challenge this exercise is addressing?
- Imagine that a quick, radical transformation in the direction suggested by this exercise might be possible. What might that transformation look like?

23 Calmness Switch

When you enter the room that is your mind, make sure to flip on the switch by the door. This turns on the lights. This gesture can also accomplish a second thing: it can produce instant calmness.

Our anxiety, our agitation, and our racing brain prevent us from living the life that we would like to live. We can't visit our favorite faraway places if we're afraid to fly. We can't live our dream of performing if we're too anxious to perform. We can't make our best decisions if our brain is racing and our nerves are jangling. Achieving needed calmness exactly this simply, by flipping a switch, will help you achieve your other mental health goals.

Maybe you can't change your anxious nature or eliminate all the distress and agitation arising from past traumas by engaging in a single mental exercise of this sort. But if you want to change your anxious nature and reduce that agitation you will have to pick a starting point and this is a wonderful place to start. Whenever you enter the room that is your mind, turn on the lights—and at the same time, by virtue of having flipped that switch, feel calmer.

Explain to yourself, "It is odd but I think I get this idea, that I can become genuinely calmer just by deciding to become calmer." When something happens to raise your anxiety level today, whether it's a problem at work, something you encounter in the news, a problem with your current creative project, some family matter, or one of your chronic pestering thoughts, take a deep breath and say, "I am practicing calmness. Let me flip that calmness switch and deal with this calmly."

This is a simple, excellent way to manifest your love for yourself and to more powerfully stand behind your own life-purpose choices. When we allow ourselves to be pulled around by the nose by our own frayed nerves, boiling blood, and racing brain, we aren't able to be the person we intend to be. More calmness is a bedrock value that promotes all the other values we want to uphold.

- When that hunger builds up in you to eat anything and everything and throw your diet out the window, say, "I am practicing calmness. Let me flip that calmness switch and deal with this calmly."

- When that particular thing that your mate does that always drives you crazy is about to drive you crazy for the millionth time and provoke a fight that you know will lead nowhere, say, "I am practicing calmness. Let me flip that calmness switch and deal with this calmly."
- When the novel you're writing stalls because you don't know what happens next, instead of badmouthing yourself or abandoning the project say, "I am practicing calmness. Let me flip that calmness switch and deal with this calmly."
- When that craving builds up in you to start drinking, do all the things you know to do as part of your recovery program and also say, "I am practicing calmness. Let me flip that calmness switch and deal with this calmly."
- When you feel that terrible heaviness and emptiness because life has suddenly lost all meaning, when you know that the deep sadness that dogs your heels is about to descend on you, rather than rushing off manically to do something, anything, to forestall that feeling and rather than taking to your bed and pulling the covers up over your head, say, "I am practicing calmness. Let me flip that calmness switch and deal with this calmly."

In each case there is more to do than just be calm. Calmness alone will not keep you from overeating, improve your relationship with your mate, allow you to finish your novel, ward off a drinking binge, or keep existential sadness completely at bay. But it is a valuable first step and may even make all the difference.

You can increase the calmness in your life in many ways. Thinking thoughts that calm you rather than agitate you is beneficial. Removing stressors from your life will help. A useful relaxation technique or a simple breathing technique will also help. But nothing is simpler than creating a calmness switch that you learn to flip when needed in the direction of calmness. You can associate this idea with our metaphor of "the room that is your mind" by having the switch that flips on the lights in that room double as a calmness switch. Give it a try!

Primary Issue: General Anxiety and Agitation

- What other issues might this exercise help address?
- How might you personalize and customize this exercise?
- What are five thoughts that would align with and support this exercise's central intention?
- What five actions might you take so as to support any changes
- How might you put your imagination and your native brilliance to customize this exercise, upgrade your personality, improve

your experience of indwelling, or meet the challenge this exercise is addressing?

- Imagine that a quick, radical transformation in the direction suggested by this exercise might be possible. What might that transformation look like?

24 Non-Magnifying Glass

Maybe there's some big thing that you know that you need to do. Maybe it's changing your job, separating from your mate or stopping your drinking. This thing feels so huge, dangerous, and consequential that you can't get anywhere near tackling it. You have the thought "I hate my job!", bite your lip, dismiss the thought, and proceed on with your life.

The habit to learn is to tolerate such thoughts for more than a split second. Just that. Just practice tolerating a thought like "I need to begin dating again" or "I need a divorce" or "I need a new line of work." Notice the barrage of thoughts and feelings that assault you as you try to maintain that thought. Implore yourself to stay with the process.

When you try to hold a thought like "I need a divorce!" you're likely to be assaulted by "If I leave him I'll suddenly be poor!" and "I've never worked in my life" and "I'll feel like such a failure!" and "Children of divorce have so many problems!" and "What will I say to my priest!" and "My parents will give me such a look when I tell them" and "I'll need a job!" and more. Try not to shut down. Try to keep tolerating the thought "I need a divorce!"

It may feel horribly hard. So many upsetting consequences may flood your mind. But in order to make the changes that you need to make in life the first step is tolerating thoughts. Don't worry about "doing anything" with any thoughts and feelings that flood you as you try to stay with a given difficult thought. You don't have to dispute them, answer them, handle them, accept them, or anything. You just have to survive them. You just have to tolerate them.

The activity of tolerating them creates calmness and an opening. You begin to see that you can survive the thoughts and feelings that come with thinking difficult thoughts. Decisions and action steps may come next. Whether or not they come, this is nevertheless the habit to learn: tolerating a difficult thought. You've been setting up the room that is your mind to make it as safe and congenial a place as possible for thinking and feeling.

Begin to reap the benefits of that outfitting by using your redesigned room as a safe haven for tolerating difficult thoughts.

A corollary useful habit is to not magnify difficulties. We cause our own distress if we magnify the difficulty of our tasks. Our tasks are already real: there is no need to magnify them. Our language should not make hills into mountains. Making mountains out of hills is a habit to avoid. Refusing to add incendiary language to our everyday self-talk is a habit to cultivate.

If as a painter I say, "Let me call that gallery," I have added no unnecessary distress to an already charged task. If, however, I say, "Let me call that gallery, but where did I put that number, and I'll probably get a machine, but what if I get a person, what would I say then, and I'm not sure I really want that gallery, but if I don't get it I won't be represented anywhere, and that means I have no career whatsoever", I have worked myself up and made it much more likely that I won't call. If I do manage to call, it's likely that I'll handle the call poorly, having agitated myself so much.

Why do we magnify our difficulties? We magnify them for all sorts of understandable reasons. Maybe our tasks feel that difficult. Maybe it pleases us to see ourselves burdened by the sorts of difficulties that only a warrior hero could meet. Then, when and if we manage to handle such "huge" difficulties, we boost our ego. Maybe there is some emotional payoff to feeling ourselves victimized, beleaguered, or put-upon. Maybe life feels boring and we crave the dramas we create when we pour fuel on what are small fires. These are common, completely human reasons for engaging in a practice that fails to serve us.

Practice the habit of not magnifying difficulties. You do not need to shrink difficulties and act as if they do not exist. Just don't magnify them. Picture possessing a magnifying glass that does not magnify but that simply allows you to see what is there. Imagine how an ant would look through that sort of glass. Imagine how an everyday task would look. The ant looks tiny, probably so does the task. Get in the habit of using a non-magnifying glass! Make sure to include that among the tools you keep in the room of your mind. Even if there is some payoff to turning ordinary difficulties into huge internal dramas, the downside is significantly greater.

Big change is hard and trying to think about big change may be even harder. Bringing up difficult thoughts creates whirlwinds and hurricanes. Learn how to bravely weather those storms. By doing so you give yourself a better chance to make the changes likely to improve your emotional health. One key is not magnifying your difficulties: to maintain a proper perspective, make sure to employ your non-magnifying glass!

Primary Issue: Tolerating Difficult Thoughts and not Over-Dramatizing Difficulty

- What other issues might this exercise help address?
- How might you personalize and customize this exercise?
- What are five thoughts that would align with and support this exercise's central intention?
- What five actions might you take so as to support any changes you consider important to make?
- How might you use your imagination and your native brilliance to customize this exercise, upgrade your personality, improve your experience of indwelling, or meet the challenge this exercise is addressing?
- Imagine that a quick, radical transformation in the direction suggested by this exercise might be possible. What might that transformation look like?

25 Resilience Mat

The many ups and downs of the creative life are extremely challenging. Managing to endure them and bounce back from them require real resilience. What can help? The mat you install in the room that is your mind, the mat from which you get up from again and again.

You might picture it as a yoga mat, a gym mat, or any sort of mat you like. When some powerful blow strikes, when you are laid low by circumstances, when you fail yourself in some small or large way, visit the room that is your mind, settle yourself onto your resilience mat, shut your eyes, breathe deeply, and get up again.

Often, in order to get off the mat, some forgiveness will be required. Who or what are you forgiving? Lars, a coaching client, explained to me:

> I need to forgive everything. I have a tendency to immerse myself in too many facts about the world, bringing weight, inertia and opacity to my reality. All that heaviness makes it almost impossible to act or to create. It has dawned on me that an all-encompassing forgiveness is the first step in dissolving my heavy reality and opening myself up for creativity. I must forgive everything, not only my failures, so that my laboriously collected thoughts, experiences, sorrows, rules, habits, perceived limits, etc., are liberated. I understand this liberation as a form of generosity in my relationship with myself.

Dynamic self-regulation and healthy indwelling require the sort of conscious liberation that Lars describes, an all-encompassing forgiveness where you forgive yourself, others, and the world for the sake of rejuvenating yourself, freeing up the energy that is being held as sadness and despair, and allowing the motivation to create to bubble up. You are saying, "Without turning a blind eye, I am forgiving everything for being exactly what it is so that I can return with renewed commitment to my life purpose choices." Then you get up off the mat.

The resilience that we require is in large measure existential. We have made ourselves sad and ineffectual by virtue of taking in several centuries' worth of the deconstruction of everything. But that belief, that we do not matter and that our efforts do not matter, is a mental mistake. The mistake sounds like the following: "When I was young I wanted life to be a certain awesome thing. Now I see that it isn't. Therefore, it is nothing much at all."

Once you understand that the meaninglessness you are experiencing is an artifact of wishful thinking about a universe you believed ought to exist and once you accept the reality of this precise natural world, created as a result of natural forces and without the sort of purposefulness or fairness you want for it, then you can get on with making meaning and creating a life that matters—not to the universe but to you.

To do this you will need to change your mind about what you need life to be—objectively purposeful, part of a cosmic plan, watched over by unseen eyes or guided by some unseen hand, and so on. Instead, you will want to hold on to a different vision, that you do not need to be happy, that you do not need to move mountains, but that you *do* need to make yourself proud by engaging in value-based meaning-making. Getting off the mat is the physical analogue to reminding yourself that your life is in your hands and that, existentially speaking, you are obliged to continue with the project of your life.

This exact creature that we are *can* make meaning, but only in ways that a human being can make meaning: that is, with the knowledge that *it* is doing the making, that *it* has made a decision about life, and that nothing out there is monitoring that decision, smiling or frowning about that decision, or caring about that decision. Maybe you wanted life to mean something more than that or different from that. But that desire, which is the exact equivalent of a negative evaluation of life as it is, helps maintain sadness and meaninglessness.

We are obliged to muster resilience in the face of all sorts of challenges—poor health, relationship difficulties, creative missteps, hurricanes, meaning crises, and all the rest—and a powerful step in rebounding is ceremonially picking ourselves up off the mat. To do that, it can help to have a mat. Off in a corner of the room that is your mind, lovingly ready if and when it is needed, is that mat. When you're struck a blow, use that mat to help you recover.

Primary Issue: Insufficient Resilience

- What other issues might this exercise help address?
- How might you personalize and customize this exercise?
- What are five thoughts that would align with and support this exercise's central intention?
- What five actions might you take so as to support any changes you consider important to make?

- How might you use your imagination and your native brilliance to customize this exercise, upgrade your personality, improve your experience of indwelling, or meet the challenge this exercise is addressing?
- Imagine that a quick, radical transformation in the direction suggested by this exercise might be possible. What might that transformation look like?

26 Meaning Fountain

Since meaning is a certain sort of psychological experience, like all psychological experiences it comes and goes. The bad news is that it can go. The good news is that it can come back. We can have the experience of meaning again, especially if we actively "make meaning" by engaging in activities that we previously experienced as meaningful and by making sure to live our life purposes and our values. Since meaning can and does return, the following is true about meaning.

Meaning is a deep, inexhaustible wellspring and an infinitely renewable resource. Today it may not seem meaningful to sit by the pond and feed the ducks, as you have too much you want to do; sixty years from now—or tomorrow, for that matter—you may decide that sitting by the pond for an hour or two is abundantly meaningful. At nine in the morning the meaning that springs to mind might be to fight an injustice; at ten, to send your daughter at college a sweet note; at eleven, to work on the song you're writing; at noon, to stretch and write for another hour; at one, to pass on meaning and pay some bills; at two, to resume fighting that injustice; and so on. There is always more meaning available.

To think of meaning as something to find—something like a lost wallet or a lost ring—is to picture meaning as a very paltry thing. In that model, meaning is so small a commodity that you can acquire it by attending a guru's lecture or by sitting cross-legged in a dark room. You weren't sure what was meaningful—a guru speaks—now you know. Really? No, meaning is nowhere out there; and, if it were, that would make it a tiny, trivial sort of thing. What if you were informed by a booming voice that the meaning of life was to stand on one foot while singing show tunes? Would that impress you or work for you? I hope not.

Bob, a client, explained to me:

> I know nothing about ultimate reality and I'm certain that no one else does either. But I recognize that some things feel meaningful to me and even consistently meaningful. If this is true, that is the same thing

as saying that meaning is available to me. It may not be available to me at all times, in all moods, or in all weather, but I embrace the idea that meaning is a renewable human resource. More than that, I can take charge of it bubbling up. This may sound strange in words but I know what I mean. I know how to accomplish this feat of restoring the meaning flow in my life.

Marcia, a client, explained to me:

> As I began to really see that meaning is a wellspring I felt more connected, hopeful, empowered. I felt a sense of not only connecting to a particular meaning-making choice, but to a deeper awareness of the limitlessness of possible meanings and choices. I found myself at times visualizing journeying into a wellspring deep in the earth, traveling through time, traveling and shape-shifting into the awareness and viewpoints of other people, of animals, of trees, of energies that had taken a drink from the wellspring; they were like little creation stories. As soon as I internally agreed that meaning was a wellspring it not only shifted my understanding of meaning-making but brought on a lightness as well.

Susan, a client, put it this way:

> Conceptualizing meaning as a wellspring changed my relationship to meaning. Like Old Faithful, the famous Yellowstone geyser, I began arriving at my desk with a bubbling up of energy. I experienced a building sense of creativity during the days when, because of my other responsibilities, I couldn't get to my writing; then, on the days when I could, I found myself able to stay put for much longer periods of time. The image of an inexhaustible wellspring helped me maintain meaning on the days when I couldn't get to the computer and it helped me make meaning on the days when I could. It seemed to work on many levels, to deepen my connection to my creative work, to banish existential depression, and to help me do the ordinary, everyday things more lightly and effortlessly.

Add a courtyard to the room that is your mind. In that courtyard, install a gurgling fountain. Decide on its look: a fountain from Rome, a fountain from Seville, a fountain from your imagination. This fountain represents the truth that meaning is a wellspring and that meaning is always available. If you are having a boring day, if you are having a sad day, if you are having a meaningless day, head directly to that lovely courtyard and to your meaning fountain and stand reminded that meaning, while it can vanish, can also return. Enjoy the play of light on water and feel meaning return.

Primary Issue: Counteracting Meaninglessness

- What other issues might this exercise help address?
- How might you personalize and customize this exercise?
- What are five thoughts that would align with and support this exercise's central intention?
- What five actions might you take so as to support any changes you consider important to make?
- How might you use your imagination and your native brilliance to customize this exercise, upgrade your personality, improve your experience of indwelling, or meet the challenge this exercise is addressing?
- Imagine that a quick, radical transformation in the direction suggested by this exercise might be possible. What might that transformation look like?

27 Drama Royalty

To the world, you may look very sedate. You may reply calmly when addressed, measure your words, run errands without making a fuss, and appear angst-free. Yet in that room that is your mind, you may be playing out so many dramas that it's fair to say that you're addicted to drama.

Most people are. Most people are terribly addicted to drama—without even knowing it. What does this addiction look like? Here are four typical self-created dramas that I encounter when I coach creative and performing artists.

You're a writer. Someone you know says that she'll be happy to read your just-completed manuscript. You send her the manuscript. She replies that it turns out that she is too busy to read it. From this relatively trivial event you create the most intense, dramatic, exclamation-point-littered drama about betrayal, humiliation, failure, and the essential cruelty of the universe. Why would a writer do that and derail herself for six months, a year, or forever? Chalk it up to our human penchant for careless overdramatizing.

You're a painter. You've finished some new paintings and you're not sure what to charge for them. You have good reasons for charging what you usually charge, you have good reasons for increasing your prices, and at the same time you could try charging almost any amount under the sun, from next to nothing to some outlandish amount, given the extraordinary range of prices for paintings. Rather than make some choice—any choice—you turn this everyday difficulty into dramatic paralysis and stop selling and stop painting. You throw up your hands and descend into despair.

You're a singer/songwriter. You've written some new songs and want to record them. But you're not sure which ones to record. This one sounds nicely commercial—but is it too commercial? This one is very arty—but is it too quiet? This one is excellent but really requires an accompanist—but who's available? This one is catchy—but doesn't it vaguely sound like somebody else's song? You stew about this and keep raising the heat under the pot until the stew is boiling. Should it be this song, that song, or the other song? This song, that song, or the other song! Finally, the dramatic explosion that was coming arrives and you table your project indefinitely.

You're an actor. Your current headshots have you with short hair. But you think you look better with long hair. So, you schedule a pretty expensive photo shoot. The day goes poorly, in part because you're not thrilled by the way you look, in part because the photographer doesn't seem sympathetic to your requests. You get the results of the photo shoot. Not one picture thrills you. Some are serviceable—but is serviceable good enough? You throw an internal fit, about wasting all that money, about now having no headshots you like, and about the absurdity of the life you're leading. As a result, you avoid auditioning for the rest of the year.

You may not look like a drama queen or a drama king to the world. But something happens when you enter the room that is your mind. There, the moment you arrive, you are handed permission from yourself to throw a fit, upset all the furniture, and act as if your world has crashed into a million pieces. An engraved invitation was waiting and you accepted it. Why? Well, maybe life felt a little boring and you craved some excitement, even of this unfortunate kind. Maybe this was the straw that broke your back. Maybe you're furious about something else and this was a convenient trigger. Who can say? Whatever the reason for accepting it, you did.

Since this invitation is waiting for you, you'll need to prepare yourself for it right off the bat. First, pin a sign on the door to the room that is your mind: "No drama royalty allowed." Second, enter that room very carefully, watching out for invitations. If an invitation is waiting, thrust at you on a silver tray by a butler in livery, shake your head and murmur, "Ah, no, you've mistaken me for a diva." Third, stay alert as you move about: some drama may be lurking behind the armoire or under the cushion of your easy chair, waiting to pounce.

Some part of us is inclined to exclaim at the drop of a hat, "The world has offended me!" If we were kings or queens, we'd lop off some heads. Not being royalty, we swallow that outrage and transform it into paralysis and self-sabotage. Wouldn't it be ever so much better not to play out that drama in the first place? Engrave on your easy chair, "This is not a throne." Put up little signs everywhere: "No dramas, please." Maybe that will make your room a little less exciting—but that's the wrong kind of excitement anyway.

Primary Issue: Reducing Inner Self-Sabotaging Theatrics

- What other issues might this exercise help address?
- How might you personalize and customize this exercise?
- What are five thoughts that would align with and support this exercise's central intention?
- What five actions might you take so as to support any changes you consider important to make?

- How might you use your imagination and your native brilliance to customize this exercise, upgrade your personality, improve your experience of indwelling, or meet the challenge this exercise is addressing?
- Imagine that a quick, radical transformation in the direction suggested by this exercise might be possible. What might that transformation look like?

28 Beauty Drawer

Very important is the chest of drawers that you install in the room that is your mind. You will have many uses for it. To begin with, one dedicated drawer will be your beauty drawer—the subject of this exercise—where you keep reminders of your essential beauty and talismans that ward off and help you heal the virulent self-criticism that may be plaguing you.

I find it important to remind participants that they each have an immaculate center or core that is their essential nature. Our thoughts may be very far from beautiful as we pester ourselves, plot our revenge, wax snide and ironic, complain about life, and in countless other ways darken our own doorstep. Our actions may likewise prove anything but beautiful as we indulge an addiction, fail to show up to our life purposes, squander meaning opportunities and behave far below our own standards. But, often quite hidden away and sometimes almost impossible to access, is that essential loveliness—that humanity, that beauty, that goodness—with which every infant enters the world.

You can better access that splendid core by taking a daily trip to that chest of drawers that you've installed in the room that is your mind, opening the drawer in which you keep your beauty talismans, and reminding yourself that you are not your thoughts, not your feelings, not the you who was manic today or chaotic today or despairing today or terrified today, not the you who ate too much at lunch or passed the buck at work, but the you who shares genetic wealth with everyone who has ever done the right thing and risen to the occasion.

What will your beauty talismans be? You can have many, given that you have a whole drawer available! One might be a photo of you at four or five, impish, happy and perfect, getting ready to dive into the lake or cut your birthday cake. A second might be a poem you love, one that captures the poignancy of living, written out in your own hand and decorated like a page out of an illuminated manuscript. A third might be a marble that represents your precious core. What else? You can have so many! Create your own wonderful collection of talismans and mementoes that do the right job of reminding you that you are fundamentally precious.

I recently strolled a path surmounting the white chalk cliffs of the English coast and thought about the D-day armada that sailed off to liberate Europe. There will be pitched battles and bloodshed until the end of time and the horrors arising out of our human inheritance may ultimately overwhelm the beauty that is also a feature of that inheritance. In the big picture of armies and tidal waves, what is a marble or a poem or a photo of you at five? What are they? They are just about everything, really. They inspire you to be your best self and to do the next right thing. What else matters more than that?

How might you use your beauty drawer? You might open it every morning as part of your morning routine: you pick out your actual clothes and then you visit the room that is your mind, open your beauty drawer, visit with your talismans, take one or two out to touch and hold, and announce, "I am the beauty in life" or something similar. Then, later in the day, maybe when you've done something just a little bit foolish or disappointing, you visit with them and they help you heal. Then, in the evening, as part of your bedtime routine, rather than having some anxious thought or some resentment be the last thing on your mind, you visit your beauty drawer and fall asleep while gazing at your talismans of worth. Wasn't your day enriched by having spent real time with your richest self?

The theme of this lesson is what is known as disidentification, an idea made popular by the Italian psychiatrist Roberto Assagioli, the developer of a branch of psychotherapy known as psychosynethesis. Assagioli explained:

> We are dominated by everything with which our self is identified. Some people get their identity from their feelings, others from their thoughts, others from their social roles. But this identification with a part of the personality destroys the freedom which comes from the experience of the pure "I."

I am picturing this "pure you" as really beautiful—and maybe even as civilization's saving grace. Remember it, keep it alive, and access it frequently by visiting your beauty drawer daily.

Primary Issue: Reducing Self-Criticism and Increasing Self-Esteem

- What other issues might this exercise help address?
- How might you personalize and customize this exercise?
- What are five thoughts that would align with and support this exercise's central intention?
- What five actions might you take so as to support any changes you consider important to make?

- How might you use your imagination and your native brilliance to customize this exercise, upgrade your personality, improve your experience of indwelling, or meet the challenge this exercise is addressing?
- Imagine that a quick, radical transformation in the direction suggested by this exercise might be possible. What might that transformation look like?

29 Power Bars

Many even quite competent people do not have their demonstrable competence translate into self-confidence. They squirm and wriggle in the room that is their mind and say things like "I can't do this" and "I'm not equal to that" and "I surely better not try that other thing!" As a result, they live a reduced life and may even forfeit their dreams. They do not write their novel, they do not start their business, they do not push physics forward. They get many things done quite nicely—but not the most important ones.

How terrible! But what if they had a lovely array of mental power bars to munch on that provided lots of energy and renewed confidence? Wouldn't that prove quite the blessing? Let's add those power bars to your mental arsenal! Remember that chest of drawers from the last exercise? Let's line one drawer with some prettily patterned shelf paper and stock it with all sorts of power bars. You get to pick your flavors. How about peanut butter chocolate? Oatmeal raisin walnut? Hard and crunchy? Soft and chewy? Can't you taste them already!

You also get to design the wrappers and name your brand of confidence. What will you call these power bars? Maybe "Super confidence boost!" or "I can absolutely do this!"? You design the logo, pick your colors, select your graphics, and create an array of confidence boosters that are not just tasty but that are also beautiful, beautiful like a gorgeous label on a wine bottle or an exquisite box from an upscale chocolatier. Go ahead and create your product line and stock your pantry right now!

How might you use these power bars? Here's an example. Say that you have a long-standing dream. Say that your dream is to build an online business that works so well and produces so much income that you can travel anywhere you like and hop around the world. You're aware that some people are doing this, you know that you're pretty skillful, savvy, and resourceful, and the only thing standing in the way is … what exactly? What has kept you from pursuing this dream of yours?

Well, many things. It all seems so vague and confusing. And you don't have a solid idea for your business. And there are so many come-ons with hefty price tags guaranteeing that with no effort you too can make millions online—those come-ons really turn you off. Plus, a paycheck is a paycheck. Plus, you don't have the time, the energy, the tech skills, the connections or the … or the anything! But, of course, it all comes down to a failure of nerve and a shortfall of confidence. So, instead of pursuing your dream you throw in the towel for another day, another week, another month, and another year.

Don't do that. Don't give up on your dream because your confidence failed you. By all means, don't spend those thousands of dollars on suspect online trainings. But also, don't throw up your hands. And certainly, don't dismiss your idea as ridiculous or beyond your reach. Instead, grab a confidence bar. Go to the room that is your mind, open the top drawer where you keep your power bars, take a moment to survey your spectacular array—the champagne and dark chocolate ones, the gooey nougat ones, the ones that you got at the little shop on the rue de Bac—and choose your power boost.

Unwrap it slowly. Take a bite. Savor the taste. Feel your confidence rising. Feel the boost. Use that burst of energy to propel you to do something in the service of your dream. Maybe that something is just walking, breathing, and thinking. Maybe that something is making a list. Maybe that something is finding free Internet information from generous dreamers who have made their online business dreams work. Use that power bar boost of confidence to do something in the service of your dream. And if your confidence slips, have another bar! Along with their other miraculous benefits, they contain no calories. You can nibble on them as often as you like without gaining an ounce!

The mind is the place where we lose our confidence. Our knees may buckle or our throat may tighten, but that's because our mind weakened those body parts. The mind is also the place where we can regain confidence. We can say things to ourselves that serve us and that support us. We can say, "I have an excellent novel in me and I'm going to write it" or "I'm going to make that online business work and finally move away from here!" And if you feel that confidence waning? You know what to do. Go directly to that drawer marked "Eat me!" and grab a bite of confidence.

Primary Issue: Lack of Self-Confidence

- What other issues might this exercise help address?
- How might you personalize and customize this exercise?
- What are five thoughts that would align with and support this exercise's central intention?
- What five actions might you take so as to support any changes you consider important to make?
- How might you use your imagination and your native brilliance to customize this exercise, upgrade your personality, improve your experience of indwelling, or meet the challenge this exercise is addressing?
- Imagine that a quick, radical transformation in the direction suggested by this exercise might be possible. What might that transformation look like?

30 Wallpaper

Right behind your everyday thoughts and feelings, even when those thoughts and feelings are relatively light and friendly, may reside a constant background coloration of sadness. That's true for a great many people.

For a vast multitude, it's as if they'd painted the walls of the room that is their mind the most depressing shade of gray imaginable; or as if soot from a coal fire had continually deposited itself on those walls since they were little. What can be done about all that background sadness?

Well, new wallpaper, of course! First let's get those walls prepped. Let's get all that soot off! Fire up your power washer and power clean those walls. Watch all that soot disappear down the drain. Lucky that you can power wash your walls without getting anything wet! There go a lifetime of regrets and disappointments. There go the failures, there goes the harm done to you, there goes the sludge of missed opportunities and broken promises. Isn't it quite something to see those walls clean again?

Now, as your walls dry, let's pick out your wallpaper and get that sadness packing. Pull out some gorgeous imaginary wallpaper books, sit in your easy chair, and peruse the patterns: the floral ones, the Victorian ones, the graphical ones, the ones that remind you of Mondrian, the hypermodern ones, the Gothic ones, the super simple ones, the ornate ones resembling cake decorations. What shall it be?

Which cheers you up the most and warms your heart? That's the one!

Hanging real wallpaper is no easy feat. But hanging this wallpaper is a breeze! Watch it go up without a wrinkle or a bubble in sight. While you're at it, throw open your windows and let a good breeze in. And if wallpaper doesn't do it for you, then paint your walls some colors you love. Create exactly the bright, cheerful walls you want. This is your room and you can paint it or wallpaper it any way you like!

There's more to do, too, in addition to putting up new wallpaper or painting your walls, if you want to get rid of a lifetime of sadness. Let's summarize a bit. In the first exercise, you installed windows so as to let in a breeze, some fresh air and some fresh thoughts. Throwing open those windows will help with the sadness. In the third exercise, we got rid of your customary bed of nails and introduced an easy chair—surely that easy chair makes for a happier mental environment. In various exercises, we've created ways for you to deal with the return of traumatic memories, we handled painful feelings, and we dealt with anxious thinking. In Exercise 13 we threw a lovely mind party so as to banish despair. All of this will help reduce that background coloration of sadness.

Each of these efforts will help you improve the landscape of your mind. Together, they amount to something like a program, an odd, eclectic program based on the simple but true idea that your mind is a kind of place where you dwell. You can construct and decorate the room that is your mind as you choose, even now after a lifetime of repetitive and negative thinking and despite all the stiffness and stuffiness that comes with your formed personality. You can do this!

The major shift I'm suggesting is the shift from the idea that you are merely a creature who thinks thoughts to the truer idea that you are a creature who can enter into a brilliant, dynamic relationship with your own brain. By employing the metaphor of a room that your lively imagination creates, by visualizing that room and its contents, and by stocking it with what you need and deserve—bright walls, an easy chair, windows that open, and all the rest—you keep yourself mentally healthy.

Most people live in a cell and are their own jailer. You do not need to live like most people. You can switch out that prison cell for a room as pleasant, as beautiful, and, yes, as functional as you would like to make it. Rather than living in the place that your formed personality created and commanded that you inhabit, you can live in a new, comfy place that your available personality wants, knows it needs, and loves to visit. There are no movers to hire, no remodeling costs, no months of dust, debris, and upheaval. You just use your imagination, completely for free.

Welcome to the room that is your mind. I hope you like the wallpaper you chose—and if you don't, switch it right out! You can do anything here, anything you like and anything that serves you, and you can do it in an instant. Your brain is a great imagination machine: imagine your best mind into existence and live there happily and well.

Primary Issue: Persistent Low-Grade Sadness

- What other issues might this exercise help address?
- How might you personalize and customize this exercise?
- What are five thoughts that would align with and support this exercise's central intention?
- What five actions might you take so as to support any changes you consider important to make?
- How might you use your imagination and your native brilliance to customize this exercise, upgrade your personality, improve

your experience of indwelling, or meet the challenge this exercise is addressing.

- Imagine that a quick, radical transformation in the direction suggested by this exercise might be possible. What might that transformation look like?

Part III
30 Cognitive Strategies for Increased Creativity

31 Blazing Fire

In this Part I intend to present exercises that are geared to the needs and challenges of smart, sensitive, creative individuals, especially those who self-identify as creative and who work as, for example, writers, inventors, painters, research scientists, software engineers, composers, etc. We'll continue to use the metaphor of "the room that is your mind" and examine thirty exercises with the power to increase your creativity, help you meet the challenges of the creative life, and promote your emotional wellbeing.

Although it might seem self-evident that a smart, sensitive, creative individual would feel naturally motivated to engage in his creative work, in reality the majority of creatives and all would-be creatives find it hard to maintain motivation. For one thing, the work is arduous and comes with knotty intellectual and creative challenges, and for another, only a percentage of it will prove good (and only an even smaller percentage excellent), for a third, whatever they produce is open to criticism, rejection, dismissal, pushback, and scrutiny; and more. It is much harder to maintain motivation to work creatively than one might at first glance imagine.

Indeed, that motivation can vanish entirely. An infant is motivated to cry when it's hungry but if you fail to attend to that baby often enough he will lose his motivation to cry, fall into despair, "fail to thrive," and may even die. That lack of response to his cries saps his motivation to keep crying and can even sap his motivation to live. What if a novelist keeps sending out her novel and no one will publish it? Can she maintain her motivation to send it out or maintain motivation to work on her second novel? Can she thrive?

That ignored infant loses his taste for living and his desire to live. A creative person can lose her taste for creating, her desire to create, and even her desire to live, for a long laundry list of reasons. Therefore, it is on her shoulders to pay attention to this issue and to find ways to maintain motivation in the face of that laundry list of challenges. When that flame starts to dwindle, she must pay attention to that dwindling and stoke the fire. If that fire goes out completely, she must relight it and rekindle the flame.

Whatever else she does in order to rekindle her desire to create, it would be smart if she also installs a fireplace in the room that is her mind, builds a blazing fire in that fireplace, and warms herself there. At some deep level that surpasses understanding and that must connect to our most primitive instincts, a blazing fire in a fireplace means something to us: it sparks our imagination as much as it warms our hands and our feet.

Keeping a fire perpetually lit in that fireplace, moving her easy chair near it, and warming herself there are among a creative person's most important tasks, because to the extent that she is cold and unmotivated, exactly to that extent will she experience tenacious creative blocks and massive resistance to creating. Rather than bad-mouthing herself about not creating or pestering herself as to why she is not creating, the better plan is for her to announce, "I'm feeling cold and unmotivated and a fire will help!"

She can use that fire in other ways as well. It is the place where she can write out her regrets on small pieces of paper and burn them. She can burn rejection letters from literary agents and gallery-owner refusals to mount her work. She can read the memoir she's working on in that loving, flickering firelight. She can daydream and fantasize there. It is the place that makes her easy chair feel all that much cozier while serving as her prime reminder that motivation can wax and wane and even die out—and she mustn't let that happen.

Picture the room that is your mind. You have an easy chair already installed; install your fireplace opposite. Have a lovely supply of logs arrive. Have plenty of kindling materialize. Start a lovely fire and begin to enjoy it. Announce to yourself, "This fire warms me and motivates me and enables me to get on with my work." Sit for a while, enjoying the beauty and warmth of the fire, and at a certain point, maybe sooner rather than later, move to your desk or your easel and launch into your work.

When desire wanes, it's hard to face our creative work. When that spark dies completely, it's almost impossible. You can help yourself keep the flame of desire alive in all sorts of ways but one profound way is to install a fireplace in the room that is your mind, keep a fire blazing there, and, like someone in the wilderness who must keep her fire going, demand of yourself that you will pay attention to your fire and that you won't let it flicker out.

Primary Issue: Lack of Motivation

- What other issues might this exercise help address?
- How might you personalize and customize this exercise?
- What are five thoughts that would align with and support this exercise's central intention?
- What five actions might you take so as to support any changes you consider important to make?
- How might you use your imagination and your native brilliance to customize this exercise, upgrade your personality, improve your experience of indwelling, or meet the challenge this exercise is addressing?
- Imagine that a quick, radical transformation in the direction suggested by this exercise might be possible. What might that transformation look like?

32 Snow Globe Collection

It's hard for creative ideas to percolate up if your mind is too noisy. A noisy mind is exactly the equivalent of countless unnecessary thoughts grabbing hundreds of millions of valuable neurons and stealing them from the good work they might otherwise be doing. As many billions of neurons as we have, a single thought grabs a substantial number of them, robbing us of our full intellectual powers.

If you are busily thinking that the lawn needs mowing, that you hate your day job, that you've already used up all of your vacation time this year, that your child is beginning to bite other children in his preschool class, and that your oven, which needs cleaning, is not self-cleaning, it is highly unlikely that you will also be solving the difficult plot points in your novel. Where would those plot-point solutions come from if billions of your neurons were already engaged in all that thinking?

There are many different ways to conceptualize that noise and to actually reduce that noise. The practices of mindfulness and meditation are currently popular ways of dealing with all those thoughts, some of which do not need to be thought and just need to be quieted, and some which must be indeed be thought—you do need to address and problem-solve your two-year-old's biting habits—but not in such a self-pestering, obsessive way that it prevents you from creating.

Another frame for the quieting you want to achieve is anxiety management. It may well be the case that the majority of that noise—that many of those neuron-stealing thoughts—are the nattering results of ambient anxiety. If they are, then calmness is the answer. Growing calm can produce the quiet you require in which good ideas have the chance to percolate up. There are many sorts of anxiety management strategies you might try so as to achieve this calmness, but the following is a great one to employ in the room that is your mind.

Create a lovely snow globe collection and keep it on top of the dresser that in a earlier exercise you added to the room that is your mind. When you want to quiet your mind and calm yourself, go to the room that is your mind, select one of your snow globes, shake it up, and as the snow settles feel yourself settling and growing calmer and quieter. When life is swirling around you, when your own thoughts are swirling inside of you, when you can hear nothing but agitated noise in your own mind, go directly to that room, select a snow globe, and use it to help you settle.

You might employ a single snow globe that you use regularly to calm yourself or you might enjoy creating a whole snow globe collection, adding to it periodically, and becoming a snow globe collector. When you travel, come upon a Christmas market in an Alpine village, and encounter some charming Bavarian snow globes, add one or two to your mental collection. This activity of collecting snow globes keeps them in mind, reminds you of their value, and reinforces the idea that you know exactly how to calm yourself when your mind grows too noisy, perfectly enjoyably with a snow globe and a smile.

You might adopt this snow globe exercise or ceremony as one of the first things you do whenever you enter the room that is your mind. Let it become your entrance ritual, the first thing you do as soon as you arrive. You've designated a certain time to write your novel, create your app, or compose your symphony; as noisy as you are feeling, you still manage to send yourself to the room that is your mind; as soon as you get there, select a snow globe, give it a vigorous shake, and, as the snow inside of it settles, feel yourself settle. You might think of doing this first thing every time.

Give it a try right now. Create your first snow globe. What scene shall you choose? Maybe a quaint Alpine one? Maybe one with the Eiffel Tower at the center? Maybe a cozy Christmas fireplace scene? Maybe one related to the creative work you do: maybe a symphony orchestra, if you're a composer, or a starry night, if you're an astronomer? Create your first snow globe—it won't be your last, since, if you feel like it, you can create a whole collection of them—shake it up, watch the snow settle, and feel yourself growing calm and quiet as the snow settles.

Maybe you're a glass artist capable of fabricating snow globes. Not only might you create your own customized snow globes for your own use, you might also create a line of snow globes for sale and promote their calming powers. If you're an application designer or a virtual reality designer, you might create (and sell) a calmness application or a calming environment that operates on the same principles that make snow globes such powerful calming tools.

If you don't love the first snow globe you create, try creating another one. What could be simpler! Create a few based on the books you've written, on elements in the periodic table, or on places you've traveled. Try a variety out. There's no cost—and some unlikely one may prove your calming charm!

Primary Issue: A Too-Noisy Mind

- What other issues might this exercise help address?
- How might you personalize and customize this exercise?
- What are five thoughts that would align with and support this exercise's central intention?
- What five actions might you take so as to support any changes you consider important to make?
- How might you use your imagination and your native brilliance to customize this exercise, upgrade your personality, improve your experience of indwelling, or meet the challenge this exercise is addressing?
- Imagine that a quick, radical transformation in the direction suggested by this exercise might be possible. What might that transformation look like?

33 Altar

Most human beings are not as disciplined as they would like to be. Creatives are no exception. As a result, they often bad-mouth themselves about their lack of discipline—when in fact discipline may not be the issue. More likely the issue is a lack of devotion. There is a devotional quality to the creative act, a deep regard for and love of the work, that allows a creator to continue creating day in and day out even when life is hard and even if the work is recalcitrant. If that devotion isn't there, resistance and blockage follow.

Luciano Pavarotti once explained, "People say I am disciplined, but it is not discipline, it is devotion, and there's a big difference." There is a big difference. Discipline is an excellent commodity and anyone attempting to live her life-purpose choices and create or perform needs a good measure of it. But if you aren't also devoted to your own efforts, if you don't see their merits and their value at a deeper level than mere utility or interest, it will prove very hard to spend a lifetime struggling with a tangled problem in physics or to spend four years slogging through the writing and rewriting of a complex, recalcitrant, unwieldy novel. Devotion as well as discipline is needed to pull off such feats.

What can help in this regard is the creation of a devotional altar that supports your intention to stay devoted to your work. For me, the idea of an altar has no particular spiritual connotations but is rather a visual aid in support of our human ability to love and respect deeply. I respect and love humanist ideals and traditions and have a way of including a miniature Magna Carta as part of the altar I always have available in the room that is my mind, along with a postcard of a Paris café scene and other objects and images that hold meaning for me.

Go to the room that is your mind. Look around. Where might you place your altar? You might place it on top of your dresser, next to your coffee mug collection (see 36 Mug Collection). You might place it on your work desk next to your computer. You might place it on a plant stand next to your easel. You might place it on the mantel above your fireplace, if the mantel is wide enough—and no reason why it can't be, given that every aspect of this room is in your control. Pick a location for your altar, one that will keep it very present in your consciousness.

Next, decide what your altar will include. It can include absolutely anything that you feel connects to the devotion you feel for thinking hard and well and for creating beautifully. You might include a dusty book from a bygone age, a handsome slide rule, a gloriously colorful photograph of a distant nebula, a miniature of the Bill of Rights, a relic from a meaningful trip you took, your daughter's baby shoes—anything at all. Arrange your altar exactly as you would like it to look, including its lighting, and step back. Does it suit you?

Now experience it. Feel connected to your work. Feel connected to your traditions. Feel connected to your intentions. Feel connected to what you consider important. Feel connected to your personal, idiosyncratic, individualistic vision of life. Experience the feeling of devotion. Notice how everyday distracting, disturbing, and pestering thoughts dissolve in the presence of this devotion. Feel suffused with this unmistakable, invaluable, incontrovertible feeling.

Because your altar exists in the room that is your mind, you can change it whenever you like. Maybe on one visit it'll resemble a room in the British Library. Maybe on another visit you'll populate it with spring flowers. Maybe sometimes it'll have an ancient feel to it, maybe sometimes a hypermodern feel. You can conceptualize your altar either way, as permanent as a pilgrimage site or as changeable as light through the day. What matters is that you feel devotion well up in you as you encounter it.

To what are you pledging your devotion? See if you can articulate that devotion. Articulating your devotion will help you design your initial altar. Remember your goal: to maintain motivation and to meet the many challenges that come with the creative act, the creative process, and the creative life by standing devoted. The altar that you create in the room that is your mind will help you maintain that stance.

Primary Issue: Insufficient Devotion

- What other issues might this exercise help address?
- How might you personalize and customize this exercise?
- What are five thoughts that would align with and support this exercise's central intention?
- What five actions might you take so as to support any changes you consider important to make?
- How might you use your imagination and your native brilliance to customize this exercise, upgrade your personality, improve your experience of indwelling, or meet the challenge this exercise is addressing?
- Imagine that a quick, radical transformation in the direction suggested by this exercise might be possible. What might that transformation look like?

34 Speaker's Corner

Freud suspected that all cases of writer's block were instances of self-censorship. It wasn't that the writer didn't have words or ideas, but that for some reason he was afraid to express them and share them. Self-censorship is indeed a huge issue for all human beings, creatives most definitely included. This truth helps explain why public speaking is the world's number one phobia: most people are made profoundly anxious by having to speak in public and reveal something about themselves.

Even if their talk has nothing to do with them personally—even if they are presenting company sales statistics—they are still revealing how good or how poor a job they are doing at organizing their thoughts, sounding cogent and coherent, and so on. Their presentation may be about sales statistics but *they* are on full display. Think of how much truer this is for a research scientist contemplating presenting a controversial theory, a painter contemplating a suite of antisocial paintings, or a novelist contemplating writing a novel whose theme is revenge.

What are we afraid that we might reveal? That we aren't as smart as we'd like to think we are. That we aren't as talented. That we aren't as accomplished. That our performance leaves a lot to be desired. That our writing is uninspired. That our visual imagery is trite. That we're second rate. That we're derivative. That we're disgusting. That we're behind the times. That we're childish. That we're ...

Plus, it can feel frankly unsafe to say what's on our mind. To make a political or social statement in a blog post, an essay, a book, a song, or a painting is to invite pushback, criticism, ruptures, retaliation, financial, familial, and job consequences, and even, in many places and times, imprisonment or death. It is completely reasonable to take seriously the consequences of speaking our mind. But taking those consequences seriously and deciding never to speak are too different things. The first is prudence; the second is abject silence.

What can help? A dedicated speaker's corner in the room that is your mind.

Historically, the most famous speaker's corner was the northeast corner of Hyde Park in London. But there are other speaker's corners, both in England and around the world. There are speaker's corners in Indonesia, the Netherlands, Italy, Canada, Australia, Singapore, Thailand, and elsewhere. They provide a designated place for a person to speak his or her mind—though, contrary to popular belief, not all speech is permitted there. In the speaker's corner that you create in the room that is your mind, *all* speech is permitted.

Why might you be censoring yourself? You might be a Darwin and worried about how your views on nature may be received in a dangerously religious environment. You might be a Goya and worried about how your activist paintings may be received in an authoritarian environment. You might be a James Baldwin and worried about how your homoerotic writings may be received in a virulently homophobic environment. Whatever the source of your self-censorship might happen to be, you don't want to censor yourself before you've had a chance to speak your mind, at least to yourself. Use your speaker's corner to practice speaking all things dangerous and unmentionable.

How might you design your speaker's corner? And where will you put it? Will it be an old-fashioned soap box with a megaphone? A podium with a microphone? A spotlighted stage and a hand mic? Will you put it in a corner of the room that is your mind or in some more prominent spot? Give those details some thought right now. Situate and design your speaker's corner. Then try it out! Visualize yourself standing there, speaking your truth. Picture yourself eloquent, forthright, and powerful. What do you hear yourself saying?

How might you use your speaker's corner? Say that you've been writing a novel and for some reason you've gotten stuck and blocked. That might have happened for any number of reasons, but one may be self-censorship. Go to your speaker's corner. Speak your novel's darkest, most difficult truths. See how they sound out loud. Are they indeed dark and difficult truths but not so dangerous as to be excluded? Or do they reveal too much and really must be avoided? Do your brave speaking, do your equally brave evaluating, and see what you've learned.

Maybe you'll be able to immediately resume writing your novel. Maybe you'll have learned how to revise it strategically. Maybe you'll understand why it must be abandoned. The chances are excellent that your courageous efforts will have produced some useful movement. A surprisingly hard challenge for creatives is counteracting self-censorship and courageously speaking. Creating a speaker's corner in the room that is your mind and using it to speak your mind can help end that self-censorship.

Primary Issue: Self-Censorship

- What other issues might this exercise help address?
- How might you personalize and customize this exercise?
- What are five thoughts that would align with and support this exercise's central intention?
- What five actions might you take so as to support any changes you consider important to make?
- How might you use your imagination and your native brilliance to customize this exercise, upgrade your personality, improve your experience of indwelling, or meet the challenge this exercise is addressing?
- Imagine that a quick, radical transformation in the direction suggested by this exercise might be possible. What might that transformation look like?

35 Selection Table

Creatives often have many projects in mind and many projects in progress. An independent filmmaker might be in postproduction on one film, raising money on a second film, entering a third completed film in film festivals, and contemplating several next films. A neuroscientist might be working on a popular book about the mind, a textbook about his specialty, several journal articles, and some new experiments meant to buttress his hypotheses. Often enough, this is too much to handle, resulting in one or another of the following outcomes.

Having so many choices can easily cause a creative to throw up her hands, announce that it's all too much, and end up doing nothing in support of her creative efforts. Months may pass this way, even years. Every day she knows that she ought to be doing something, anything, and every day she is making herself sad and disappointing herself by not choosing and acting, but that jumble of choices remains somehow so daunting that, despite how it is making her feel, she yet again avoids her work.

Or, so as to reduce her anxiety about choosing, she may choose one of her projects and work on it obsessively, to the exclusion of all her other projects, even though she knows that she really ought to be submitting her completed film to film festivals and tackling all of the postproduction details on her other film rather than focusing so completely on a fledgling film. The fledgling film fascinates her and she can justify her obsession with it in many ways, arguing, for example, that her mind can only successfully tackle one thing at once. At the same time, she knows that she's treating her finished film and her almost finished film unfairly.

Having too many choices results in other negative outcomes as well. Unable to choose among the many articles he might write, a would-be professor may never acquire the tenure he so desperately wants. Unable to choose among which of her images to market, a would-be graphic designer may find herself spending all her time at the service of her paying clients and none of her time building her own business. The list of negative outcomes from a painful multiplicity of choices is very long. What is a creative to do?

He must make sure to include a selection table in the room that is his mind. The table might look like a drafting table, a cleared-off desk, an antique card table, or any sort of table large enough to hold the choices in question. When, burdened by all these choices, he feels ready to throw up his hands and choose nothing, he knows to say to himself, "Selection table time," to go to the room that is his mind, to stride directly to his selection table, to lay out his choices, and to choose.

He lays out his completed film, his almost completed film, his fledgling film, and his ideas for future films and he says, "All right, what's next?" or "All right, what shall I choose for this evening?" or some other phrases meant to signify that he is not choosing for all time but choosing just for today, just for the next hour, even for just the next twenty minutes. He makes his choice and then he acts.

He goes online and submits the finished film to a film festival, however tedious that process may be. Or he gets in touch with the composer who is supposed to be scoring his almost finished film and tries to get clarity on when the score will be done, however difficult writing that email may feel. Or he gives himself the treat and pleasure of working a bit on a new idea, knowing that, because of his new commitment to careful choosing, he doesn't have to worry that working on this new idea will derail him or begin to consume him.

That is, he uses this selection table to enter into a new, less anxious, more powerful relationship to choosing. This selection table becomes one of the most important items of furniture in the room that is his mind. Maybe, before he goes to it, he uses a snow globe to calm himself or warms his hands by the fire, so as to feel his passion rekindled. Maybe he creates a ritual or ceremony that he learns to repeat: fire, snow globe, selection table. In this way, choosing stops daunting him.

Create your selection table. If you have some choice to make that you know needs your attention, use your new selection table to make that choice right now.

Primary Issue: Difficulties Choosing and Committing

- What other issues might this exercise help address?
- How might you personalize and customize this exercise?
- What are five thoughts that would align with and support this exercise's central intention?
- What five actions might you take so as to support any changes you consider important to make?
- How might you use your imagination and your native brilliance to customize this exercise, upgrade your personality, improve your experience of indwelling, or meet the challenge this exercise is addressing?
- Imagine that a quick, radical transformation in the direction suggested by this exercise might be possible. What might that transformation look like?

36 Mug Collection

Every morning I take the following pleasure. I open one of my kitchen cupboards and choose my coffee mug for the day. I maintain five or six primary choices and many backup choices. Currently my six primary mugs represent Paris, London, Prague, New York, Rome, and Berlin. The Paris mug is stenciled with the Paris Metro system. The Prague mug features the famous Charles Bridge. The New York mug features a lot of coffee iconography. It reminds me of the cafés I frequented in the West Village as a teenager.

What do these mugs do for me, in addition to holding my coffee? They remind me of my traditions. They remind me that humanist values are upheld by the few, that great ideas do not come from committees, that, just as I do, other writers have had to sit down and spend a year or two or three getting their words straight in order for fine books to exist, and that a significant handful in every time and place have thumbed their nose at tyrants and ridiculed humbug.

They also remind me of my responsibilities. I am obliged to stand with those freethinkers, humanists, and freedom fighters. Those innocent coffee mugs do a lot for me! You, too, can feel less isolated and less alone and can better maintain your motivation by reminding yourself of your traditions, either by employing a mug collection that, for example, celebrates stops on the international bohemian highway, or in some other way of your own choosing.

Which traditions are important to you? Maybe you feel yourself a part of the long tradition of Catholic writers. Maybe you feel more connected to the ancient Greeks, to Plato, Aristotle, Socrates, Democritus, and other natural philosophers of that bygone age, than to any thinkers of today. Maybe something about the lives of expat artists—women painters of the Left Bank, black musicians of the Paris jazz clubs, Russian ballerinas who danced for Diaghilev in the Ballets Russes—fires your imagination and moves your heart. If you feel connected in such ways, create a mug collection to celebrate what you're feeling.

Wake up each morning, visit the room that is your mind, contemplate your mug collection, and select a mug for the day. You may be as alone in your studio or your lab as a star in space, but you are also connected to all those souls who feel and have felt the same way that you do about jazz, short stories, or abstract math. And regularly add to your collection. There's no cost and you can't possibly run out of room!

I recently visited Brighton, England for the first time to lead a workshop there. I realized quickly that a Brighton mug belonged in my collection. Brighton struck the right chords and stirred the right emotions. Back in the 1930s, the British novelist Graham Greene frequented the pubs dotting the Lanes, the narrow shopping streets near Brighton's seafront, and dreamed up the characters who populated the world of *Brighton Rock*. You can visit the Greene room upstairs at the Cricketers and peruse the author's framed letters—or you can create a Graham Greene mug for your green tea. The latter is what I did.

In that solitude that every creative person craves and needs, you may begin to feel lonely, isolated, and alienated. Your experience of spending time in the room that is your mind can slip from exquisite to unbearable. If you find yourself thinking, "I am so alone," turn directly to your mug collection. Say, "I am not alone, I am traveling the path so many have traveled before me." Say, "I have many friends I have never met." Feel comforted by the way that, in the room that is your mind, you can embody your cherished traditions and enjoy the past's presence.

A useful coffee mug collection is not a substitute for actual human contact. You will want to supplement celebrating your traditions with actual hugs and kisses and, yes, with the actual tears and bruises that come with intimacy. But that you need that vital supplementary reality doesn't change the fact that you are not ever alone, not if you embrace your traditions. You do not need to love or respect those in your lineage—they are just people after all, with their warts and shadows. But they have toiled in the same fields as you toil and, at least with respect to this one love—their love of fiction, their love of freethinking, their love of jazz—they share and have shared your deepest values.

Create your coffee mug collection and celebrate your traditions. If you do, you will feel less alone.

Primary Issue: Feeling Isolated and Alone

- What other issues might this exercise help address?
- How might you personalize and customize this exercise?
- What are five thoughts that would align with and support this exercise's central intention?
- What five actions might you take so as to support any changes you consider important to make?

- How might you use your imagination and your native brilliance to customize this exercise, upgrade your personality, improve your experience of indwelling, or meet the challenge this exercise is addressing?
- Imagine that a quick, radical transformation in the direction suggested by this exercise might be possible. What might that transformation look like?

37 Hat Drawer

Each of us is a single self that is made up of many identities. You are a woman, a Protestant, a watercolor artist, a New Englander, and so forth. The majority of these identities are not adopted, they are simply who we are and always have been. Other identities we assume as we live, for example taking on the identity of psychoanalyst, expat or retiree. The matter of identity is almost as complicated as the matter of mind: for instance, there are at least a score of identities available to any given artist, who may see himself as more a beautifier, more a trickster, more a classicist, and so on.

Artists discover that they must adopt certain identities whether they want to or not. Creatives today are obliged to hone marketing, promoting, and entrepreneurial skills that support their creative efforts and act in public ways that artists of bygone ages did not have to act. Today a musician is as likely to have a hit because he pulls off a stunt as because he pens a brilliant ballad, as likely to be cherished for his celebrity status as for his artistry, and more cognizant of his media opportunities than his creative opportunities. A smart, sensitive, creative person is unlikely to relish these duties and may frankly hate them. This then becomes a roaring internal conflict, the conflict between what an artist wants to do—especially making worthy art—and what she is obliged to do, namely relentlessly market and promote.

It is better for a creative to embrace these tasks and these unwanted identity pieces rather than waging an inner battle with no winners. Only a certain sort of shift is required to accomplish this embrace, the shift from feeling put upon by these duties to accepting that many activities in the service of meaning do not themselves feel meaningful. This is a mature attitude worth cultivating. To help cultivate this attitude, do the following.

Designate a drawer in the chest of drawers that you've placed in the room that is your mind as your hat drawer. In it are all the hats that you enjoy wearing and that you are sometimes obliged to wear. What might this crowded hat drawer contain? The hat you wear when you want to be your wildest at the easel. The hat you wear when you want to be your most careful and get all those details right. The hat you wear as you rehearse a meeting with a gallery owner.

It might include the hat you wear as you write marketing and promoting copy for your next newsletter. It might include the hat you wear when you switch artist identities for the day and opt to spend your time painting as an abstract expressionist painter rather than as your usual representational painter. Let the drawer be phenomenally crowded with hats, so as to provide a visual reminder that you have many roles to play in life, many tasks to accomplish, and many identities to juggle.

How will you use this drawer? Say that you are well aware that it is past time to query literary agents about the novel you've just finished writing. You've been able to put off the moment of reckoning by waffling internally about whether you intend to self-publish the novel or try a traditional route, but you've known all along that you meant to try a traditional route and now you can't deny that truth any longer. Still, you've been balking—and feeling terrible. Now that you have your hat drawer available, you can try the following.

Open your hat drawer. Put on a hat you enjoy wearing. Maybe it's the hat you associate with writing in the garden or having tea with your sister. Wear that hat for a bit and enjoy the moment. Smile your enjoyment. Then sigh, if you must, and say, "Writing query email hat, please." Rummage through the drawer and find that hat. Do not disparage it. Do not make faces as you search for it, as you put it on, or as you wear it. Give it a good tug to make sure that it's on properly. And then without angst or drama work on that query email.

You really are obliged to wear many hats in life and each represents its own set of challenges, the challenges associated with, say, being a member of a minority or being a creative artist in a field that makes little money. The many hats in your hat drawer are there to make you smile and chuckle but they are also there to remind you how many tasks come with living authentically. Use your hat drawer both to bring you joy but also to remind you of your practical and existential duties.

Primary Issue: Reluctance to Market and Promote

- What other issues might this exercise help address?
- How might you personalize and customize this exercise?
- What are five thoughts that would align with and support this exercise's central intention?
- What five actions might you take so as to support any changes you consider important to make?
- How might you use your imagination and your native brilliance to customize this exercise, upgrade your personality, improve your experience of indwelling, or meet the challenge this exercise is addressing?
- Imagine that a quick, radical transformation in the direction suggested by this exercise might be possible. What might that transformation look like?

38 Life-Purpose China

It is painfully easy for a smart, sensitive, creative person to begin to doubt that he or any of his efforts really matter. Why spend so much time, sweat, energy, and blood crafting a poem? Why throw all of your intellectual eggs into the basket of string theory when string theory may prove just a passing fancy? Why turn over your whole life to literary criticism when the books you are teaching now bore you? Why provide another mental disorder diagnosis to another client when you've stopped believing in the logic or legitimacy of diagnosing? Why bother with any of this?

This common problem—a sense of lost purpose and the experience of encroaching meaninglessness—is best counteracted in the following way. You remind yourself—or perhaps inform yourself for the first time—that you do not intend to make the mistake of believing that there is a single "meaning to life" or a single "purpose to life." Rather, you are going to back the idea that there are multiple life-purpose choices that you might make and that you can do a beautiful job of identifying one of these many life-purpose choices to embrace when another life-purpose choice, like your current creative project, feels stale and empty.

If, today, writing poetry does not feel especially meaningful to you, you decide to embrace your life-purpose choice of relationship and go to the zoo with your daughter, you decide to embrace your life-purpose choice of service and volunteer your time, you decide to embrace your life-purpose choice of activism and engage in some smart work in the service of a cause that matters to you, or you decide to embrace some other life-purpose choice that feels alive and available. Then, tomorrow, you can see if returning to your poetry, your string theory, your literary criticism or your clinical practice feels less dull and beside the point. It may indeed feel less dull and pointless, having taken a vacation from it and having spent time in another meaningful pursuit.

You can help remind yourself that you know how to keep meaning afloat in the following way. Create a set of life-purpose china that you store in the room that is your mind and that you use for existential snacking. Say that writing poetry has started to feel pointless. You would go to the room that is your mind, go to the cupboard you have installed, and pull out your life-purpose china, the full set of them, the eight or ten or twelve life-purpose dinner plates that make the complete service.

Take a moment and think through what dozen motifs you want displayed on your dinner service—that is, see if you can create a menu of life purposes. On that list might be important "doing" activities like creating, relating, serving, and truth-telling and equally important "ways of being" like being calm, being passionate, or being authentic. They might include "my health," "speaking up for children," "supporting my mate's career," or "moving evolutionary theory forward." Create your list or menu now.

Next lay out the plates, each hand-painted with one of your life-purpose choices, and choose one for your upcoming snack. Maybe you'll choose your activism plate. Maybe you'll choose your mystery-writing plate. Maybe you'll choose your career plate. Maybe you'll choose your friendship plate. Maybe you'll choose your "being calm" plate. Maybe you'll choose your "being passionate" plate. Pick a plate, get out some silverware, and prepare to snack.

Bring out your scones, butter, and jams. Fix yourself a lovely snack on the life-purpose plate you've chosen. As you munch, daydream about how you intend to live that particular life purpose today. Will you take your daughter to the zoo? Ah, maybe it's too chilly for that. Then might you take her on her first visit to an art museum? That might be fun! You could teach her all about drawing outside the lines and speaking in her own voice. That would make for a lovely few hours! Go do exactly that and take her on that excellent field trip.

It is easy to forget the extent to which creating is not just about making new or beautiful things but rather represents one of our life purpose choices. It's also easy to forget that you have many other life-purposes choices available to you, in addition to creating. Your set of life-purpose china, each plate decorated with a different life-purpose choice, can provide important reminders on that score and help keep you in existential balance.

Primary Issue: Loss or Lack of Purpose

- What other issues might this exercise help address?
- How might you personalize and customize this exercise?
- What are five thoughts that would align with and support this exercise's central intention?
- What five actions might you take so as to support any changes you consider important to make?
- How might you use your imagination and your native brilliance to customize this exercise, upgrade your personality, improve your experience of indwelling, or meet the challenge this exercise is addressing?
- Imagine that a quick, radical transformation in the direction suggested by this exercise might be possible. What might that transformation look like?

39 Screen Time

We are all already looking at a lot of screens a lot of the time. But the following, although it involves screen viewing, won't tire your eyes or waste your time. I'd like you to install a sizeable screen in the room that is your mind, maybe above the fireplace where you rekindle your desire and opposite your comfy easy chair, and use that screen to view how you currently operate and how you might improve your operations.

Consider the following common problem. Creatives often leave their creative work too soon, putting in twenty minutes or half an hour and then getting anxious, confused, or defeated and abandoning their work. Maybe they get derailed by a stray thought like, "I have no idea what I'm doing!" Maybe some fear—that what they're creating isn't very good, that it won't be liked, or that it will never sell—frightens them out of the studio. Maybe some distraction from the outside world—a truck rumbling by—breaks their working trance, leaving them suddenly resistant to resuming. Whatever the reason, the spell is broken and the work ends.

Imagine that this is your problem. And imagine that, seated in your easy chair in front of a blazing fire, you could watch these antics of yours played out on the screen above the mantel. Wouldn't you shake your head in dismay and exclaim, "Wow, did I really leave that easily? I won't do that again!" Maybe some simple, brilliant solution will occur to you, for instance, "Gee, what if I just got up and stretched rather than outright fleeing? Maybe after just a little stretching and breathing I'd be able to get right back to work!"

The beauty of all this occurring in the room that is your mind is that you can use the screen above your mantel not only to watch your antics, but to view any changes you decide to make and whatever transformations occur. Now, sitting there, instead of seeing yourself fleeing the studio at the first disruptive thought, you see yourself calmly rising, stretching a bit, strolling about a bit, and—maybe even with a smile on your face—resuming your creative efforts. Wasn't that lovely to watch? And didn't it seem completely plausible?

Or, say, you want to radically change how you use your lunch break at your day job. First, watch how lunch currently goes. There you are, checking your emails and doing this and that on your phone. Now, run the reel of the lunch hour you want. There you are, standing up, striding out of the office, and making straight for the park two blocks down. The sun is shining. You sketch for twenty minutes, then savor your sushi. Then you stroll back, entranced by the light. Isn't it easier to pick the lunch you want when you see them one after another up there on that screen?

You can watch a whole day in a matter of seconds, just as in a brilliantly cut and edited film. Say that you decide that you would like to exhaust yourself in the service of your work every Saturday. You intend to work from 5 a.m. until 2 p.m. on your current suite of paintings. Using your screen, you can view how such a day might play itself out. Maybe you notice that by 7 a.m. you're already half-exhausted. What to do? Maybe that's the perfect time for a breakfast break.

Ah, but you see yourself lingering at the kitchen table, spending too much time on your phone. Well, just change that. Have yourself hop right up after that second cup of coffee rather than procrastinate with a third cup. Okay! You are back to work. What do you see next? Maybe the next challenge comes at about 11 a.m. when some dreadful fatigue overtakes you. What to do? Ah, a hot shower seems right! You take your shower and get back to work. Now it's approaching 1 p.m. and you're not sure you can get another stitch done. Well, then maybe 1 p.m. is the real outer limit, not 2 p.m. If it is, clean up and celebrate!

Use the screen above your mantel to play out both what is and what ought to be. See how you currently interact with gallery owners—and how you would like to interact instead. Watch yourself avoid completing a painting—and watch yourself completing it. Watch yourself giving an interview—and watch yourself giving a better interview. You can use the screen that you install in the room that is your mind to reality-test, rehearse, and create an upgraded version of yourself, one that, when you see it up there on the screen, makes you smile.

Primary Issue: Prematurely Abandoning Creative Work

- What other issues might this exercise help address?
- How might you personalize and customize this exercise?
- What are five thoughts that would align with and support this exercise's central intention?
- What five actions might you take so as to support any changes you consider important to make?
- How might you use your imagination and your native brilliance to customize this exercise, upgrade your personality, improve your experience of indwelling, or meet the challenge this exercise is addressing?
- Imagine that a quick, radical transformation in the direction suggested by this exercise might be possible. What might that transformation look like?

40 Mirror, Mirror

You now have a screen above the fireplace mantel in the room that is your mind. Let's alternate that screen with a mirror. I would like you to use that newly-installed mirror to watch yourself speaking. This may prove to be among the hardest things you will yourself to do in the room that is your mind. But it's an extremely important effort to make.

Creatives regularly find it difficult to describe their work to others or to powerfully advocate for their work. This difficulty lessens their chances of interesting the marketplace in their wares, whether those wares are inventions, paintings, or sonatas.

Preparing your pitches in front of the mirror you install in the room that is your mind can help you reduce your fear, your social anxiety, and your performance anxiety and can help you dramatically increase your skill level as a confident advocate for your work.

How might you use this mirror? Say that you're an art photographer with a penchant for creating macabre series of photographs. For your last series, you photographed road kill that you transported to mountain tops. The images are absolutely striking—but also off-putting to many and a hard sell to virtually everyone. Your photographs are wonderful but no one will buy them. It is your job, and no one else's job, to create language that helps you sell them, and you can accomplish this task with the help of your mirror.

Rather than complaining, "Those Philistines know nothing about art!" or stubbornly exclaiming, "My photos speak for themselves!", you visit the room that is your mind, begin by using your snow globe collection to calm yourself or your coffee cup collection to remind you of your traditions, and then murmur, "How can I use language to support these excellent photos?"

Maybe a phrase will suddenly come to you: "There are no accidents in the wild places." How interesting. Might that work? You look in the mirror and repeat, "There are no accidents in the wild places." You discover that you not only love that phrase but just like that the photo series has acquired additional meaning for you. You now have powerful language to exploit—and new marketing motivation as well.

Likewise, we feel more powerful and self-confident when we train ourselves to speak in short, crisp sentences with real periods at the end of them. If our communication style is to produce long, tortured sentences full of apologies, disclaimers and other weaknesses, it is vital that we learn to change that style and opt for brevity and power. In front of your mirror is the place to practice those crisps bits of language.

Here you might try, for example in anticipation of meeting with a gallery owner, "I have a large network of loyal admirers." Here you might try, for example in anticipation of a conversation with your mate about your right to keep creating even though your efforts aren't bringing in much money, "I will make money this year." If your mate rolls his eyes and replies, "Oh, really? How?', you reply, "By working really hard and by proving the exception." Here you might try, in anticipation of a conversation with a friend who is asking for too much of your time, "I have to paint today."

You can also use your mirror to practice telling the truth. It can be the place where you let down your guard, look yourself in the eye, and say, for instance, "I am really sad." Maybe it's been very hard to make that admission. To make it is to bring up all the areas of your life that may not be working very well, from your tiresome day job to your lack of success as a creative to your chronic problems with life purpose and meaning. Here, in front of this mirror, you bravely make that admission, sigh, and ask, "Mirror, mirror on the wall, what should I do?" Maybe what you'll receive back is a little magical advice from your wisest self.

If you're design conscious and you're decorating the room that is your mind in a particular style—French cottage, New York loft, Roman antique—then create a mirror that matches. Or let your mirror be generic. Either way, add a mirror to the room that is your mind and learn to bravely face it. Our natural defenses and our everyday resistance to practicing new habits may make this difficult, but the results—better advocacy for your creative efforts, increased self-confidence, and a powerful communication style among them—are worth the effort.

Primary Issue: Difficulties Describing and Speaking about One's Creative Work

- What other issues might this exercise help address?
- How might you personalize and customize this exercise?
- What are five thoughts that would align with and support this exercise's central intention?
- What five actions might you take so as to support any changes you consider important to make?
- How might you use your imagination and your native brilliance to customize this exercise, upgrade your personality, improve your

experience of indwelling, or meet the challenge this exercise is addressing?

- Imagine that a quick, radical transformation in the direction suggested by this exercise might be possible. What might that transformation look like?

41 Appointment Calendar

Relationships can prove problematic for smart, sensitive, creative individuals who typically struggle to retain their individuality, jealously guard their solitude, and find their healthy narcissism mixed with a good-sized dose of unhealthy narcissism. Indeed, they may even be constitutionally primed to go it alone. Still, it is harder to achieve emotional health and a measure of happiness if you don't foster relationships. Even if relating isn't a creative's first choice, it would be wise if it were a close second.

Creatives, who love to create, regularly forget that relating is also important. By forgetting to relate, they can easily become isolated, lonely and sad. A tactical solution to this common problem is to create an appointment calendar that you keep and maintain in the room that is your mind. Its literal counterpart is also necessary: there you make your actual appointments. But you'll also want to keep one in the room that is your mind, as a talisman and as a reminder that you are holding relating as something important and even vital to you.

If you're pulled to enter the room that is your mind by a pressure, by racing brain energy, by a problem that requires solving, by a creative urge, and so on, you are unlikely to think to visit your appointment calendar. But let's imagine instead that it's a dull, unexceptional day, that life feels a bit drab, and that some sadness is dogging your heels. That may prove to be the perfect moment to visit the room that is your mind, pull out your appointment calendar from the desk drawer where it resides, and wonder, "Who would I like to see?" Let the visages of the people you know parade in front of you. Include people you don't know yet but whom you'd enjoy meeting. Let that parade unfold.

Think about each person in turn, if you have the patience for that. Aunt Roberta. Cousin Tony. The woman you met at the art opening, who got your jokes and shared your likes. That friend from high school who holds some oddly important place in your memory. Your daughter who, now that she is working in the next town, you rarely see. That expert in your field whom you suppose would never deign to have a cup of coffee with you—but who knows? He does have a nice smile and kind eyes in his publicity photos. That editor who once almost published a book of yours. Your neighbor two doors down who always waves. Your father ... well, that's a tricky one, isn't it?

Maybe your answer will surprise you. Maybe it will turn out that you really would like to visit with Aunt Roberta because she, more than anyone else in the family, likes to recount family history—and it's a bit of family history that you're craving. Maybe you'll discover that you want to reach out to that expert—and more than that, that you want to propose a collaboration. Maybe it will suddenly occur to you that the editor who almost bought that book from you genuinely loved your writing style—and your new book is likely right up her alley. Who knows at what face in the parade you'll stop!

You might decide to engage with your appointment calendar in conjunction with some other ceremony we've been discussing. For instance, you might pull out your life-purpose china, choose the relationship plate, and have a nice snack on it while perusing that parade of people. If someone's face brings up a bitter memory, you might try tolerating that pain for a full ten seconds while wondering if there's something new to learn about that old story. Or you might begin by throwing open the windows you've installed and letting a fresh breeze flow through, to blow away any stray anxiety that might be building as you think about these people—each with his or her warts and shadows.

When and if you make a decision, reach out to that person. Relating is no more *the* answer to living a life of pride and purpose than is creating. But it is one of the answers. How many tremendously creative people have suffered terribly because they could not or would not love and could not or would not enjoy the company of others? Don't number yourself among those many. The appointment calendar that you maintain in the room that is your mind can help you remember that human contact is genuinely important.

Primary Issue: Loneliness and Lack of Relationships

- What other issues might this exercise help address?
- How might you personalize and customize this exercise?
- What are five thoughts that would align with and support this exercise's central intention?
- What five actions might you take so as to support any changes you consider important to make?
- How might you use your imagination and your native brilliance to customize this exercise, upgrade your personality, improve your experience of indwelling, or meet the challenge this exercise is addressing?
- Imagine that a quick, radical transformation in the direction suggested by this exercise might be possible. What might that transformation look like?

42 Crystal Ball

You may not do something very well right now. That doesn't mean that you won't do that same thing beautifully down the road. Because this is true, you want to include a crystal ball among your room's furnishings and decorations, one that you use to predict improvement and to predict success. What sorts of improvements and successes? Here's what I have in mind.

One winter evening I find myself in the green room of a beautiful new theater on the campus of the North Carolina School of the Arts, waiting to give a creativity chat to a crowd of a few hundred North Carolinians. I'd given this chat many times before, varying the title to suit the audience but presenting essentially the same material. I can now deliver it on a dime, starting up the instant you say "Go!" and ending directly on the hour. In fact, when I delivered this chat to a group of Indiana arts administrators, what impressed the conference chair the most, more than the chat's content, was the fact that I ended so promptly!

Nowadays I deliver my chat without any notes, although I keep a sheet handy with some headlines in case I blank out. This is a far cry from my early days of speaking in support of my books. In 1992, I gave my first book talk at the Green Apple bookstore, an independent bookstore in the Richmond district of San Francisco, on the corner of a street of Chinese vegetable markets and Russian bakeries. I had no clue what I was doing. It wasn't that I hadn't prepared—no, indeed—but *what* I'd prepared was wondrously odd and constituted the strangest chat that any audience has ever had to suffer through.

Instead of describing *Staying Sane in the Arts*, the book I was promoting, or, simpler yet, reading from it (as most writers on tour do), I prepared a cross between a stump speech and an academic white paper on something I called "The Artist Corps." I think I meant the speech to be a visionary call to arms on the order of "I have a dream ... for artists." It might have fit the bill if I'd been delivering it on the Washington Mall to a crowd of a million marching artists. To this small crowd, drifting in off Clement Street after shopping for snap peas and piroshkis, it was a bore and a monstrosity. To further make them wish that they had chosen the comedy club across the street, I read the darn thing, slowly (to give it weight) and softly (because I speak softly). Slowly but surely, everyone walked out.

Eventually I wandered home—but not at all crestfallen. What went through my mind was the following question: "I wonder what would work better?" It took me a while—some years—to figure that "better" out, but I knew to retire that Artists Corps speech then and there and to never dust it off again. And I got much better!

There is a six-month period during the early 1960s when Bob Dylan progressed so fast that he was unrecognizable from the beginning of the year to the end. By December his playing is a quantum leap better, his songs are a quantum leap better, even his voice, which you wouldn't think could improve dramatically, is a quantum leap better. He wasn't Bob Dylan in January. He was only Bob Dylan in December.

I, too, improved. The distance from the Green Apple chat to the North Carolina School of the Arts chat was more than a dozen years and three thousand miles. It was that non-linear distance known as a learning curve. I had learned how to speak in public. This is very important news for your creative life. You, too, can expect to improve; and that crystal ball you keep in the room that is your mind can help you see that much improved and more successful future.

If you were there at the Green Apple that evening in 1992, I pity you. I know that you would never have guessed that the stiff, boring fellow reading his speech would one day approach oratory. Fooled you! You, too, can appear one year in support of your first book and make a riotous hash of your presentations and your interviews; and then, two years later, having learned a ton, you can appear in support of your second book and look like Kennedy in Berlin. The task is not to get it right the first time. The tasks are to learn from your pratfalls, and, by learning, to improve. Your crystal ball can help remind you that this is eminently possible.

Primary Issue: Not Believing that Improvement or Success Is Possible

- What other issues might this exercise help address?
- How might you personalize and customize this exercise?
- What are five thoughts that would align with and support this exercise's central intention?
- What five actions might you take so as to support any changes you consider important to make?
- How might you use your imagination and your native brilliance to customize this exercise, upgrade your personality, improve your experience of indwelling, or meet the challenge this exercise is addressing?
- Imagine that a quick, radical transformation in the direction suggested by this exercise might be possible. What might that transformation look like?

43 Stumble Zone

Off in a corner of the room that is your mind, out of harm's way, create a stumble zone, that is, a place where tripping is likely. Maybe you'll envision it as a crack in the sidewalk or a thick watering hose or a rug designed for tripping you up. Put up a large sign in front of this stumble zone that reads, "Careful, tripping happens here!" Now, what is this all about?

Imagine that you are doing a beautiful job of maintaining your mental health and your emotional wellbeing and up comes a trip to the dentist, a visit from your mother, a broken promise by your mate, or some extra work at your job. Here it comes—that place where you regularly trip and fall.

- You know that the visit to the dentist will trigger not only panic but will completely change your personality, from the person you've been working to become to that other person who lived out of control for the whole decades of her twenties and thirties.
- You know the impending visit from your mother will create an extraordinary amount of lethargy and sadness in your system, will make you hyper-critical, and will leave you with a bad taste in your system for weeks after she's left for home.
- You know that another broken promise by your mate will create all sorts of bad feelings in you and between the two of you, including revenge fantasies, doubts about the viability of the relationship, thoughts about leaving, and a bout of severe sadness.
- You know that your job is already only barely tolerable and that when your boss springs some extra work on you on Friday afternoon, forcing you to have to catch the last train home, that will ruin your weekend, cause you to yell at your mate and your children, and almost cause you to kick the dog.

If you know from past experience that this impending event will trip you up, that means that you have good warning and can try something to prevent that trip and fall. That "something" might be anything you know to do that helps you not trip repeatedly over the very same crack in the pavement. The simplest thing it might be to visit the room that is your mind, head straight for the stumble zone you've created, halt in front of the big warning sign alerting you to watch your step—and as a result, not trip.

In recovery work this "impending event" is called a trigger. A trigger for someone who trips and falls around alcohol might be the annual holiday party at work, a visit from an old drinking buddy, or a business situation that puts him among heavy drinkers. In recovery programs, you're taught to identify these triggers, take them seriously, and know clearly what you will do when you are triggered or about to be triggered.

For someone in recovery, maybe that "something to do" is calling your sponsor or attending a 12-step meeting. Maybe it's skipping the holiday party, seeing your old buddy but only in the safety of your own home, or letting your coworkers know that you are in recovery and can't hang out with them. Maybe you would do several of these things or maybe you would do all of these things, including using the stumble zone you've created.

Picture one of your triggers—that visit to the dentist, that visit from your mother—picture it without flinching, adamantly say, "I'm not tripping there," and explain to yourself what you will do to handle that specific challenge when it looms on the horizon. We journey through life on a concrete road defined by its unevenness. The road is already buckled and will buckle more, creating innumerable chances for us to trip and fall. We will come to know some of these cracks only by tripping over them; but many of them are visible from a distance and we can prepare ourselves not to trip and fall.

Maybe we will still stumble a little—but maybe we won't stumble at all. Wouldn't that prove a welcome relief and spare you any number of bruises? Not tripping and falling repeatedly over the same challenges and obstacles is a lovely habit to learn. As much work as we may do on ourselves to keep us mentally healthy, we can still be triggered and lose our balance. When you see one of these triggers coming, take it seriously. Off to the stumble zone and the warning sign you've installed there!

Primary Issue: Repeatedly Tripping over the Same Obstacles and Challenges

- What other issues might this exercise help address?
- How might you personalize and customize this exercise?
- What are five thoughts that would align with and support this exercise's central intention?
- What five actions might you take so as to support any changes you consider important to make?
- How might you use your imagination and your native brilliance to customize this exercise, upgrade your personality, improve your experience of indwelling, or meet the challenge this exercise is addressing?
- Imagine that a quick, radical transformation in the direction suggested by this exercise might be possible. What might that transformation look like?

44 Hope Chest

When the French novelist and existential writer Albert Camus painted a smile of victory on the face of his famous character Sisyphus—Sisyphus, who had been condemned by the gods to roll stones up a mountain for all eternity but who nevertheless smiled at his predicament because he could still thumb his nose at his fate—Camus was not being true to life. In real life, human beings rarely smile when hope is stolen from them.

Human beings rarely smile in prisons, in prisoner-of-war camps, or in refugee camps. They rarely smile when they lose their children. They rarely smile when the work they do and the very prospect of work stop interesting them and they hold no hope of ever using themselves productively. They rarely smile when their body stops working well. They rarely smile when they give up hope of being treated fairly, of rising out of poverty, of making themselves proud by their efforts. In these and many other circumstances, loss of hope is most true-to-life.

What does it take to retain hope when having hope makes little sense? Few answers have worked as well as religion, where you are offered a better life elsewhere to make up for the difficulties in this one. In that better life, you will meet your slain children, the ones you can't stop mourning. In that better life, you will be finally free of pain and have everything you ever dreamed of wanting. In that better life, you can stop toiling mindlessly and finally escape oppression. Religion provides a satisfying reason for smiling now: a wonderful eternity coming.

However, what if you recognize that there are no gods, no heaven, and nothing better coming to mitigate this life? How can hope make sense then? Aren't you more inclined to drink yourself into oblivion, sleepwalk through the motions, or keep feverishly busy with one pointless enthusiasm after another rather than muster hope? Hope for what, after all?

This lack of hope serves to ruin our mental health. Existential thinkers have characteristically provided two answers to this dilemma: rebel by thumbing your nose at the facts of existence; and hope anyway, even though hope is absurd. These answers satisfy us in the corner of our being that appreciates irony and rebellion but hardly work as effective answers in the face of real feelings of hopelessness.

There isn't quite enough meat on those bones. It is hard to get out of bed just to thumb your nose and smile ironically at a universe that doesn't care one way or the other whether you have decided to get out of bed. Maybe that can prove motivation for one day out of seven—but what about the other six? If your mental health requires that you still maintain hope and if you find yourself no longer believing that hope makes any sense, what can you do?

One thing that you can try is to create a hope chest that you keep in the room that is your mind. This hope chest amounts to yet another effort—maybe a last-ditch effort—to provide a way of keeping hope afloat. Either regularly or at the very least when you are feeling hopeless, visit your hope chest, ask the question, "What in here can I still hope for?", and cross your fingers that you will land on something worth the candle. You might discover that:

- You can still hope for love
- You can still hope to love
- You can still hope for the small enjoyments that you have always enjoyed
- You can still hope to stand up for your principles and make a tiny difference in the world
- You can still hope to fight the enemies of reason
- You can still hope to wrestle something beautiful into existence
- You can still hope that your efforts will bring a few people some small comforts

Ask yourself the question, "Have I lost hope?" and honestly answer it. If you discover that you have indeed lost hope, go directly to the room that is your mind, create a hope chest, and fill it with talismans of hope. What will you include? Photographs? Quotations? Memories? Prophecies? Bark from a cherry tree? A miniature particle accelerator? Your choices can be gigantic, tiny, ephemeral, solid, anything you need them to be. This is your hope chest to fill as you require.

Be with these talismans. Losing hope happens; if you've lost hope, you have the job of restoring it. Make an effort to restore it by visiting your hope chest whenever hope evaporates.

Primary Issue: Hopelessness

- What other issues might this exercise help address?
- How might you personalize and customize this exercise?
- What are five thoughts that would align with and support this exercise's central intention?
- What five actions might you take so as to support any changes you consider important to make?

- How might you use your imagination and your native brilliance to customize this exercise, upgrade your personality, improve your experience of indwelling, or meet the challenge this exercise is addressing?
- Imagine that a quick, radical transformation in the direction suggested by this exercise might be possible. What might that transformation look like?

45 Corrective Lenses

Creatives often lose focus as they tackle a particular creative project or intellectual problem. They start with great enthusiasm on a given novel, certain in their bones that they know what their novel is all about. Then, even just a few days in, it becomes much less clear to them what they're doing. The plot has morphed; important characters have lost their significance; minor characters are wanting to take over; the setting is demanding a shift from one continent to another; little is as it was. Suddenly the very reason for writing this novel has dimmed to near invisibility.

The project has gone completely out of focus. At this point, there is a great temptation to abandon the project, which can leave a creative with a million begun things and no completed ones. To abandon a project merely because it is morphing and has gone out of focus is to abandon it too soon. To use the phrase that is now welling up—"I have no idea what's going on!"—as a reason to abandon the project, rather than to accept it as a natural feature of the creative process, is to misunderstand the nature of process. Too many creatives, and virtually all would-be creatives, over-agitated by all that morphing, abandon their work far too soon.

We can lose focus for many other reasons as well. Maybe a new project becomes insistent and asks—demands—to be worked on, causing our current project to dim and grow vague. Maybe we have to turn from our highly personal current project in order to tackle some creative work with commercial viability, so as to pay the bills. Maybe our health grabs our attention, or a serious challenge with one of our children, or the state of the world. The ways in which our current creative project can dim, lose its luster, and shift out of focus are legion.

What can help you stay focused on your current project even as it morphs and even as you're pulled away from it by life and other projects? There are many solutions; and one is employing a set of eyeglasses with corrective lens that you keep in the room that is your mind and that, when you wear them, immediately brings your current project back to mind.

Keep this pair of eyeglasses right on top of the desk you've installed and train yourself to put them on when your current project shifts out of focus.

What will you see when you put them on? Well, no corrective lens can make your current project crystal clear to you. No corrective lens can circumvent the demands and realities of process. But they can do the following: they'll remind you what you've named your project.

What you'll see when you put them on is the name of your current project in sharp, crystal clear lettering. Of course, that means that your project needs a name; and that also means that its name may change as the project morphs. The name you employ need not be the perfect name or its final name, just a clear, useful placeholder that, when you see it crystal clearly through your corrective lens eyeglasses, instantly brings the project flooding back to mind.

This naming is important in its own right. As a rule, having a working name for your project helps you remember it, picture it, understand it, and maintain motivation as you work on it. You might want to think that through right now and see if you can give your current project or the project you anticipate starting on next a working title. Once you've landed on that title, bravely let it blur and fade. Then, put on your corrective glasses. Experience the lettering instantly return in sharp focus. How exciting is that!

Use your special eyeglasses with their corrective lenses to keep you on target throughout the course of a project, from its inception to its entry into the world. Use it to help you create a body of work over time rather than a heap of abandoned projects. Yes, sometimes a project really ought to be abandoned. Maybe you know for sure that your scientific hypothesis is wrong: no need to run more experiments. Maybe you know for sure that that your current painting style is just not interesting to you: no need to produce another hundred paintings to double check. But more often than not your projects deserve to be seen on to the end, if for no other reason than to provide you with the complete experience. Toward that end, when a project grows blurry and loses focus, go directly to the room that is your mind, put on your glasses with their correctives lenses, and watch your project return instantly.

Primary Issue: Losing Creative Focus

- What other issues might this exercise help address?
- How might you personalize and customize this exercise?
- What are five thoughts that would align with and support this exercise's central intention?
- What five actions might you take so as to support any changes you consider important to make?
- How might you use your imagination and your native brilliance to customize this exercise, upgrade your personality, improve your experience of indwelling, or meet the challenge this exercise is addressing?
- Imagine that a quick, radical transformation in the direction suggested by this exercise might be possible. What might that transformation look like?

46 Appetite Artistry

Make sure that there's a place in the room that is your mind where, the second you arrive there, you get really hungry—not for food but for something meaningful to bite into, some idea, some project, some life-purpose choice. There, you want to drool. There, you want to feel ravenous. If you don't possess such a place in your being, you may end up like Kafka's hunger artist, who wasted away as a circus attraction because he could find no food that interested him.

Kafka's hunger artist, that classic sad figure from existential literature who could fast so well, spent his days starving in front of amused customers who paid to see his slow demise. From his point of view, he possessed no particular skill: it was simply that no food had ever interested him. When asked by his supervisor how he'd acquired his "admirable talent" for fasting, the hunger artist replied:

> "But you shouldn't admire it," said the hunger artist, lifting his head a little and, with his lips pursed as if for a kiss, speaking right into the supervisor's ear so that he wouldn't miss anything, "because I couldn't find a food which I enjoyed. If I had found that, believe me, I would not have made a spectacle of myself and would have eaten to my heart's content, like you and everyone else." Those were his last words, but in his failing eyes there was the firm, if no longer proud, conviction that he was continuing to fast.

Many smart people find themselves in this odd situation, firm but not proud in their conviction that there is nothing in life that genuinely interests them or that *can* genuinely interest them. They claim that they would dearly love it if something *did* passionately interest them and yet their claim sounds just a little hollow, as hollow as the hunger artist's. Is it really the case that a person in decent health and in decent spirits wouldn't find ice cream, pizza, barbecued ribs, or *something* tasty. Or is it rather that they are in poor spirits and down on life in a special way, such that their appetite has been suppressed and even ruined?

Whatever the precise reasons for this malaise, countless smart, sensitive, creative people find themselves in the position of Kafka's hunger artist, wasting away, in love with nothing, and convinced that at second glance all pursuits are bound to turn empty. Nothing seems able to provoke the psychological experience of meaning in them. They read a novel; that was okay; now what? They plant roses; that was okay; now what? They learn carpentry; they make a few objects; now what? They take a class; that was interesting enough; now what? They start a business; the stress outweighs the rewards; on to the next thing.

A person who stands as a hobbyist-in-life and bereft of meaning despairs. Yet there is some odd stubbornness to his plight, as if he is determined not to give up his worldview even if another one might come with meaning, just as addicts fiercely hold on to their addictions and will only pay lip service—or no service at all—to the idea of recovery and a life without their cigarettes, cocaine or alcohol. Many smart, sensitive, creative people become attached to both, to a life empty of meaning and to an addiction, the addiction soothing the pain produced by their stubborn refusal to take a genuine stab at making meaning.

A great many smart, sensitive, creative people entertain enthusiasms, hobbies, and interests, pursue an education and then a career, and so on, and yet never land on anything—a subject, a line of work, a life—that they feel passionate about. Even their enthusiasms, hobbies and interests bore them in short order. Here's how Sandra, a client of mine, described her situation:

> At 49, I find that I have not been able to sustain interest in anything really. Art in the broadest sense is the closest thing. I like it all but nothing really sticks. There's nothing that I'm specifically passionate about. But I wish there was. I can't help but feel that if I concentrate on one activity I will be missing out on another. Am I just greedy? Do I have the passion but not the focus? I envy artists who can explore their subjects in depth over time. It feels like I will live my whole life trying to decide what I want to be when I grow up.

No doubt each hunger artist became a hunger artist in his own way. There is no single path to a lifetime of acute meaninglessness. There are so many ways to kill off meaning: by not caring, by not committing, by not finding the courage, by not choosing, by not besting demons, by not standing up, by declaring that life is a cheat. One answer? Make sure that there is a place in the room that is your mind—a certain chair, a certain corner, a certain nook— where, the instant you arrive there, you feel ravenous. In this way, you'll cultivate your appetite, not for peanuts or Scotch or gadgets but for meaning and life purpose. Make sure that such a place exists—and visit it regularly!

Primary Issue: Lack of Appetite for Life

- What other issues might this exercise help address?
- How might you personalize and customize this exercise?
- What are five thoughts that would align with and support this exercise's central intention?
- What five actions might you take so as to support any changes you consider important to make?
- How might you use your imagination and your native brilliance to customize this exercise, upgrade your personality, improve your experience of indwelling, or meet the challenge this exercise is addressing?
- Imagine that a quick, radical transformation in the direction suggested by this exercise might be possible. What might that transformation look like?

47 Seven-Word Corner

A painter came to see me. She explained that her husband, who had recently retired early, kept visiting her in her studio space to chat about inconsequential matters. I asked her to craft a sentence of seven words or fewer that communicated what she wanted to say to him about the preciousness of her painting time and space.

Her first efforts were grotesquely long, apologetic, and weak. Finally, after many tries, she arrived at: "I can't chat while I'm working." "Can you say that to him?" I asked. "Yes," she replied. "How does that feel?" I continued. "Very, very scary."

Next, we role-played a situation she was having with the fellow who did some printing work for her. He was the only person in her area equipped to do this printing work and she liked both the work he did and his prices. But he was always inappropriate with her, saying things like "You know, I have feelings for you" and "Most husbands don't understand their artist wives."

"What do you want to say to him?" I asked. Having just practiced, she was now quicker to respond. "I need you to stop that," she said. "I am coming here to have prints made, period." She laughed. "That's two sentences, and one's a little long. But that's the idea, right?" "That's exactly the idea," I agreed.

You manifest your confidence by saying strong, clear things. Saying them in seven words or fewer is a great practice. Here are some examples of responses of seven words or fewer that a person is unlikely to make unless he's done a bit of practicing. The phrases I have in mind are in bold.

- Someone drops you an email saying that she loves your work, though she can't afford to buy any of it. Typically, you might reply with a "Thank you" and leave it at that. The new, bolder you might reply, "Thank you. I wonder about the following. **Might you tell your friends about me?** I'd appreciate that!"
- You're at a party, you find yourself chatting with someone about your art, and you have your usual difficult time explaining what it is you paint. The effort to explain yourself exhausts you and you have the sense that you haven't done a very good job of it. In such situations, it isn't likely that you're going to find

some bold note to end on. However, you indeed manage a bold note and say, **"Would you like to visit my studio?"** Rather than presuming that you've made a hash of your explanations, you propose a visit.

- Your sister asks you if you can take over minding your aging mother since "you don't have a job." You could meekly agree and lose several years of your life or you could say, **"My painting is real work."** Then you might continue, "Let's work out something equitable among all us kids, since we all have jobs and lives."

- You meet someone who says that her blog for new mothers is very popular. You might reply, "Great!" or you might reply, "Great! **Might your peeps be interested in me?**" Probably she is going to reply, "Gee, I don't know, offhand I wouldn't think so," to which you reply, "Yes, I understand, but let me tell you why they just might."

- You get an email from an artist you know announcing his participation in a group show. You could congratulate him or you could congratulate him and ask, **"Room for one more in the show?"**

- You read a blog post in an online magazine about something tangentially related to the subject matter you paint. You could nod to yourself and move on or you could drop the blogger an email and say, "Loved your post on firehouses! My art is right up that alley! **Care to do a piece on me?"**

Not being bold makes everything harder. One way to practice boldness is to visit the seven-word corner you've created in the room that is your mind and spend some time creating short, strong declarations for various occasions. Likewise, when you have the feeling that you're about to reply meekly or weakly, take a mental moment, visit your seven-word corner, craft a bold reply, and return with it. You may be surprised to discover how many opportunities to act boldly and speak boldly are presented to you. Be sure to take them!

Primary Issue: Not Communicating Strongly

- What other issues might this exercise help address?
- How might you personalize and customize this exercise?
- What are five thoughts that would align with and support this exercise's central intention?
- What five actions might you take so as to support any changes you consider important to make?
- How might you use your imagination and your native brilliance to customize this exercise, upgrade your personality, improve your experience of indwelling, or meet the challenge this exercise is addressing?
- Imagine that a quick, radical transformation in the direction suggested by this exercise might be possible. What might that transformation look like?

48 Identity Pledge

Say that you intend to be a filmmaker. That means that you are obliged to internally identify as a filmmaker. If you don't identify as a filmmaker—if you don't raise your hand when someone says, "Who in the room is a filmmaker?"— you're that much less likely to actually make films. It's crucial that to all of your other identity pieces—your identities as a woman, a Jew, a Bostonian, a Francophile, an opera lover—you add the identity of filmmaker.

Create the identity pledge "I am a filmmaker!" and murmur it as you enter the room that is your mind. Or shout it out like a warrior's cry as you leave that room to go about your filmmaking duties. In addition to employing your identity pledge, make sure to do all of the following. They will help you strengthen your identity as a filmmaker:

- Get in the habit of publicly saying "I am a filmmaker." Just as it is powerful and useful for an alcoholic to say "I am an alcoholic" publicly and out loud at an AA meeting, it is likewise powerful and useful for a filmmaker, even one who hasn't made films yet, to say publicly, "I am a filmmaker." When someone asks you what you do, say "I'm a filmmaker" rather than "I sell shoes at Macy's." There is a world of difference in these two ways of identifying yourself. The first allows you to think about film and talk about film and network about film and *be* a filmmaker. The second does no such thing.
- Prepare answers to the questions that, when put to you, cause you to lose your will to call yourself a filmmaker. One such question might be, "Have you made any films yet?" A second question might be "Would I have seen any of your films?" A third might be, "Do you make full-length films or just shorts?" Bravely articulate the questions that bother you, embarrass you, weaken you, or stop you—and create answers. For instance, to the question "Have you made any films yet?" your prepared answer might be, "I'm working on one right now on the theme of immigration—care to invest in it?" That'll turn the tables, won't it!
- Notice if and when your filmmaker identity begins to weaken or vanish. This happens characteristically when you've spent too much time not operating

as a filmmaker: that is, as the months go by and you neither plan films nor make films. During those sad months, it is entirely likely that you will begin to think of yourself less and less as a filmmaker. You want to notice that this is happening, even though it is painful to notice, admit to yourself that your identity is eroding, and engage in self-talk that boosts your identity back up. This is a time for lots of shouting of your identity pledge!

- Know what to do when you think that you've lost your right to call yourself a filmmaker because you haven't made a film in five years, because your last film was roundly panned, because you have to pay for making your films yourself, etc. None of these events should lose you your right to call yourself a filmmaker—that will only happen if you let it happen. When you feel as if you've lost that right, what will you do? At the very least, resume saying, "I am a filmmaker!" internally and publicly. Know *exactly* what you are going to do when you feel your right to call yourself a filmmaker slipping away.

- *Do* the various things that a filmmaker does. This means more than just the obvious "make films." It means understanding how films get made both from a technical standpoint and a financial standpoint. It means forming working relationships with people who can help you. It means learning to use language in rhetorically strong ways so that you make your films sound interesting to investors and audiences. It means understanding how to audition actors and understanding how to work with casting directors. It means wooing rich people and learning how to negotiate the moneyed class. It means engaging in apprenticeship activities that serve you. These are the sorts of things that filmmakers do—to solidify your self-identification as a filmmaker you will want to do them too!

- Make the support of your filmmaker identity a daily practice by paying attention to it morning, noon, and night—or even every time you enter the room that is your mind. Maybe that ought to become the password phrase that allows you entry into the room that is your mind: "I am a filmmaker." There may be days when you don't work on your film but there should be no days when you don't feel like a filmmaker. You want daily contact with your filmmaker identity, you want to know on a daily basis whether or not you are manifesting that identity and, if you aren't manifesting it, you want to take some immediate action to manifest it. *Be* a filmmaker every day and *support your identity* of filmmaker every day.

Primary Issue: Insufficiently Strong Self-Identification

- What other issues might this exercise help address?
- How might you personalize and customize this exercise?
- What are five thoughts that would align with and support this exercise's central intention?
- What five actions might you take so as to support any changes you consider important to make?

- How might you use your imagination and your native brilliance to customize this exercise, upgrade your personality, improve your experience of indwelling, or meet the challenge this exercise is addressing?
- Imagine that a quick, radical transformation in the direction suggested by this exercise might be possible. What might that transformation look like?

49 Anxiety Vows

Anxiety is a feature of the human condition and of daily life—and a much larger feature than most people realize. A great deal of what we do in life we do in order to reduce our experience of anxiety or in order to avoid the experience of anxiety. Because life can feel dangerous in all sorts of ways—from walking down a dark alley to giving a two-minute talk at work—and because anxiety is a feature of our warning system that alerts us to danger, anxiety is a prominent feature of daily life.

Our quite human defensiveness is one of the primary ways that we try to avoid experiencing anxiety. Maybe we deny what we're experiencing, try to rationalize away what we're experiencing, misname what we're experiencing as sickness, weakness, or confusion, get angry at our mate so as to have something else to focus on, and so on. We are very tricky creatures in this regard. It would be good if we did a better job of frankly accepting our anxiety and then managing it, but most people are more inclined to react defensively than forthrightly when it comes to anxiety.

We are also wonderful creatures who have it in us to create. "Creativity" is the word we use for our desire to make use of our inner resources, employ our imagination, knit together our thoughts and our feelings into beautiful things like songs, quilts, or novels, and feel like the hero of our own story. It is the way that we manifest our potential, make use of our intelligence, and embrace what we love. When we create, we feel whole, useful, and devoted. Unfortunately, we often also feel anxious as we create or as we contemplate creating. The anxiety that is such a prominent feature of human nature can and does prevent us from creating.

Why do we get so anxious around creating? There are many reasons. We can get anxious because we fear we may fail, because we fear we may disappoint ourselves, because the work can be extremely hard, because the marketplace may criticize us and reject us, and so on. We want to create, because that is a wonderful thing to do, but we also don't want to create, so as to spare ourselves all that anxiety. That is the profound dilemma that confronts and afflicts countless smart, sensitive, creative souls.

What should creatives do instead of fleeing the encounter or managing their anxiety in ineffective or unhealthy ways (say, by using alcohol to calm their nerves)? They should acknowledge and accept that anxiety is a regular feature of the process, assert that they won't allow it to derail them or silence them, and demand of themselves that they practice and learn effective anxiety management skills.

It is too big a shame not to create if creating is what you long to do. There is no reason for you not to create if "all" that is standing in the way is your quite human, very ordinary experience of anxiety. The thing to do is to become an anxiety expert and get on with your creating. What can help in addition to mastering some anxiety management skills? The following. Create an anxiety vow in which you pledge not to let anxiety silence you. Create it—and use it!

Your vow might sound something like the following. "I will create, even if creating provokes anxiety in me. When it does provoke anxiety, I will manage it through the use of the anxiety-management skills I am learning and practicing!" Or maybe the shorter, crisper "Bring it on!" Create your anxiety vow, visit the room that is your mind, bring up a creative idea to ponder, see if any anxiety wells up—and if it does, use your anxiety vow to quell it. Whenever the anxiety associated with the creative process wells up in you, and in addition to whatever other anxiety management strategy you're employing, ceremonially vow not to be derailed by it.

Since both creating and not creating produce anxiety, you might as well embrace the fact that anxiety will accompany you on your journey as a creative person. Just embracing that reality will release a lot of the ambient anxiety that you feel. Return to your current creative project right now with a new willingness to accept the reality of anxiety. Since anxiety accompanies both states—both creating and not creating—isn't it the case that you might as well choose creating?

Primary Issue: Acknowledging and Managing Anxiety

- What other issues might this exercise help address?
- How might you personalize and customize this exercise?
- What are five thoughts that would align with and support this exercise's central intention?
- What five actions might you take so as to support any changes you consider important to make?
- How might you use your imagination and your native brilliance to customize this exercise, upgrade your personality, improve your experience of indwelling, or meet the challenge this exercise is addressing?
- Imagine that a quick, radical transformation in the direction suggested by this exercise might be possible. What might that transformation look like?

50 Sitting on Your Hands

The easy chair that you've installed in the room that is your mind serves all sorts of purposes. One is that it is the place where you sit on your hands. Rather than impulsively responding to what you perceive to be a slight from the world, rather than angrily chewing out a critic, rather than doing something that you *know* will require that you undo it the instant you hit send, you visit the room that is your mind, comfortably ensconce yourself in your easy chair, and temporize by sitting on your hands.

Imagine that you're a visual artist and that you have an ongoing relationship with a "difficult" gallery owner—let's call him Jim—who, for no reason you can identify, always tries to make you feel small and wrong in your interactions with him. You have no idea why he's chosen a passive-aggressive approach to life, you suspect that he is very different with customers than he is with you, and you also suspect that he would deal at least marginally differently with you if your work sold better in his gallery. Be that as it may, you do value your exposure in his gallery—while also hating interacting with him. How do you preserve a decent working relationship in these circumstances?

First, you want to look in the mirror. You have a nice one already installed in the room that is your mind and you want to make sure to use it. The first thing we need to do is make sure that we aren't the main source or a significant part of the problem. Not infrequently we get into the habit of interacting from our shadowy side—from our insecurities, from the part of us that feels one down or disappointed with our lack of success, from the part of us that "just isn't going to take it anymore"—and by acting in such ways we make life that much harder for ourselves. Many creatives (like all human beings) alienate their peers and their supporters by interacting poorly with them. Be wiser and more careful than that.

Make sure that you are not making matters worse by virtue of having adopted a negative or confrontational attitude. If you need to say something important to Jim, be direct and clear but try not to deliver your message in a spirit of criticism or from a place of negative energy. Opt for some genuine fellow-feeling and some good graces, along with some straight talking. Our first job—and the place where presumably we have the most control—is to make sure that we are not contributing to the problem. Do your part well.

Second, learn to temporize. Learn to sit on your hands. When you and Jim interact, try not to react too precipitously. Try to temporize and maintain a little calming distance between hearing from Jim and responding to Jim. If you get an email saying that he intends to hang only two of your paintings rather than the four he previously committed to—and the email comes with a gratuitous critical dig ("Of course, if you sold better I'd hang all four, but as it is I think that even two might be a stretch")—the first thing that you want to do is not hit "reply."

If you like, you can write a nasty reply filled with every curse word you've ever heard—and then discard it.

Take a deep breath. Do something calming. Go to your snow globe collection and engage in that calming ceremony. Take out your life-purpose china and remind yourself of all the bigger things in life that are more important than this minor slight. Most of all, sit on your hands. Instead of impulsively reacting from a hurt or angry place, take your time and decide how you want to react. You might want to bite the bullet, not react at all, and respond in an innocuous way: "Two will be a great start! And when those two sell you'll no doubt want to hang the other two."

Think through to what extent calling Jim on his rudeness or his "betrayal" really serves you. Base your decision on reason and pragmatism, not on impulsivity and hurt feelings. When you make the decision to visit the room that is your mind and engage in some dynamic self-regulation and some healthy indwelling, you are providing yourself with the opportunity to pace yourself, calm yourself, and do what is best for yourself.

Maybe a compulsion is growing strong. Maybe an unproductive obsession is brewing. Maybe a lightning quick reaction is rising up in you. Now you know what to do. Temporize. You've created many ways to temporize as you indwell: the one I'm suggesting in this exercise is learning to sit on your hands in your comfy easy chair and let the drama evaporate.

Primary Issue: Responding Too Impulsively

- What other issues might this exercise help address?
- How might you personalize and customize this exercise?
- What are five thoughts that would align with and support this exercise's central intention?
- What five actions might you take so as to support any changes you consider important to make?
- How might you use your imagination and your native brilliance to customize this exercise, upgrade your personality, improve your experience of indwelling, or meet the challenge this exercise is addressing?
- Imagine that a quick, radical transformation in the direction suggested by this exercise might be possible. What might that transformation look like?

51 Costume Closet

To what extent ought you to be your "real self" in your public interactions? Think of the elementary school teacher who has learned that to maintain order in her classroom she must adopt a certain stern attitude until December. She would love to smile in September but she knows better. Like that elementary school teacher, you may have very good reasons to adopt a public persona that is different from your everyday or in-studio persona.

There are two ways to think about your public persona. One is that adopting a public persona is a way to practice "doing better" in public than you typically do in private. You might craft a public persona that allows you to exhibit more confidence than you actually feel, be clear when in your own mind you feel fuzzy, ask pointed questions that you avoid asking if you were only having a conversation with yourself, and so on. In this sense, your public persona can reflect the changes that you would like to make to your personality.

On the other hand, maybe you are quite happy with who you are "in private" but you recognize that your irony does not play well in public, that your frankness tends to be received as brusqueness, and that the qualities you take pride in have to be modulated or moderated in a public setting. In that case, you can create a strategic public persona that matches "what the world wants" and that allows you to interact effectively with, if you're a visual artist, customers, collectors, framers, gallery owners, media representatives, and the other people with whom you must interact.

Janet, a painter, explained to me:

> Whether by nature or nurture, I am a shy person who prefers to spend her time in the studio and who will do almost anything to avoid marketplace interactions. This way of being suited me better when I was learning my craft, as I really did need to focus on what was going on in the studio. But now that I have a body of work—an overflowing body of work—I need to step out into the world in ways that I find strange and uncomfortable. I have to make myself do it—it does not come naturally.

I actually have a checklist of the qualities that I want to manifest that I keep by the computer, so that every email I send out is coming from my public persona and not my shy studio personality.

Jack, a sculptor, told me:

> I've been in recovery for eight years now. Before that, when I was actively drinking, I always led with my temper. I had an attacking style—I would interrupt you, contradict you, fight you over every detail and the smallest perceived grievance, and always get in the last word. I was angry all the time, which was maybe a good thing with respect to the sculptures, as they had a lot of angry energy to them, but which was not good anywhere else in my life. Over these eight years of recovery I've cultivated a way of being that is more temperate, centered, and essentially gentle. Actually, I'm really still as hard as nails and people really ought not to cross me; but that part of me is kept under lock-and-key and almost never appears in public.

Creating a public persona is a useful exercise and a smart enterprise. Give some thought about who you want to be in public. Then imagine what that public persona would wear. Next, go the room that is your mind, create a spacious closet, and fill it with all the clothes—you might think of them as costumes—that your public persona might need. Now you know what to do when your public persona is required. You'd visit the room that is your mind, open that closet, dress yourself appropriately for the world, and then act in character.

An artist's public persona is the thoughtful, measured presentation by the artist of those qualities that she has identified will serve her best in the public arena. What qualities would you like to lead with in your public interactions? How would you like to be perceived? What public persona would allow you to advocate for your work most effectively? Build that persona—and then outfit it with a full wardrobe. Give it hats, shoes, gloves, and outfits for every occasion! The world is a place of conventions and obligations: construct a you who will do well in the world.

Primary Issue: Lack of a Functional Public Persona

- What other issues might this exercise help address?
- How might you personalize and customize this exercise?
- What are five thoughts that would align with and support this exercise's central intention?
- What five actions might you take so as to support any changes you consider important to make?
- How might you use your imagination and your native brilliance to customize this exercise, upgrade your personality, improve your

experience of indwelling, or meet the challenge this exercise is addressing?

- Imagine that a quick, radical transformation in the direction suggested by this exercise might be possible. What might that transformation look like?

52 Straitjacket Storage

If you're smart, sensitive, and creative you're likely to want to manifest all that potential. But the modern world is designed to restrict your options and straitjacket your efforts. There is no contemporary category of "general thinker" that matches the ancient job title of "natural philosopher," where one could do science, philosophy, art, and anything else that caught one's fancy. Nowadays you must do something smaller than that.

A smart person today must become a clear something—a college professor specializing in the early works of Melville, an engineer specializing in bridges, a lawyer who knows the ins and outs of tax law, and so on. Having become that something he must stay right there, trapped needing to prepare another journal article, ponder another bend in the river, or familiarize himself with another tax code change. How existentially debilitating is that!

Marilyn, a biological researcher, explained to me:

> The journey to get where I am today as a biological researcher at a prestigious university was long and hard and because it was so hard, with so many hurdles to jump over and hoops to jump through, I never noticed exactly what was happening. I never noticed that in some of my undergraduate classes I was actually excited by the material and actually enjoyed thinking about the big questions but that as each year progressed and as I had to narrow my focus, find my niche, and choose my life form, as it were (I've ended up an expert on a certain worm), I stopped thinking and spent my days in pretty dreary fashion trying to find some enthusiasm for my own research. Biology is amazing; and yet it has all come together in a very disappointing way.

Martin, a philosophy professor, described his situation in the following way:

> I've spent the last two months defending a journal article I wrote about praise and blame in Kantian ethics, defending it from the three peer reviewers who nitpicked my article to death. In order to have a chance

to get it published I need to address every one of their trivial concerns—and the problem for me isn't so much that I'm spending all of my time on what feels like a silly and mind-numbing task but rather that this is the box I've put myself in, this exact box, where I make some fine logical or linguistic distinctions and then have to act like that matters, like I am increasing human knowledge or something.

The academy is a comfortable place to be and I suppose that I could turn myself into someone who does think bigger than I currently think. But I don't. I don't know what the problem is: if it's the system, if it's philosophy itself that I don't believe in, if it's a lack of genuine interest in thinking, if it's a lack of confidence, if it's a fear of biting off more than I can chew, or what. All I know is, can I really do this for twenty or thirty more years? That seems completely unbearable.

What can you possibly do if this is the sort of challenge you're facing? A step in the direction of a possible solution is the following. Physically remove that straitjacket that is forcing you to work small and think small. Like Houdini, slip right out of it. Go to the room that is your mind, hop over to the closet where you are storing your winter overcoat and your public persona costumes, wriggle out of your straitjacket, and store it away.

You may have to put it back on when you go back to the lab tomorrow but for this evening you can wander anywhere in biology you like. You may have to put it back on tomorrow when you're obliged to defend your article on Kantian ethics but for this evening you can think as broadly as Plato, Aristotle or one of the pre-Socratic philosophers you admire so much. At the very least, you'll be able to spend a few blissful, unbound hours. Enjoy them and revel in them!

The challenges that smart, sensitive, creative people face when it comes to finding meaningful employment, surviving dull, routine work, avoiding a lifetime in a claustrophobic corner of a given profession, choosing between work that pays and work that interests them, and generally adapting their smarts to the contours of society's configurations are never-ending. You may prove to be one of the lucky ones, make an excellent match, and never feel straitjacketed. As likely as not, however, you will find yourself among the majority of smart people who perennially find that the world is designed to restrict their thinking and restrain their talents. If you are among this multitude, at least you can remove that straitjacket for some hours at a time and, for those hours, breathe and think freely.

Primary Issue: Feeling Constrained to Think Small

- What other issues might this exercise help address?
- How might you personalize and customize this exercise?
- What are five thoughts that would align with and support this exercise's central intention?

- What five actions might you take so as to support any changes you consider important to make?
- How might you use your imagination and your native brilliance to customize this exercise, upgrade your personality, improve your experience of indwelling, or meet the challenge this exercise is addressing?
- Imagine that a quick, radical transformation in the direction suggested by this exercise might be possible. What might that transformation look like?

53 Shoes of the Other

Here's another use for your closet, in addition to its function as the place where you store your straitjacket, hang your winter overcoat, and keep your public persona costumes. It can also be the place where you keep many pairs of shoes that help you empathize with the folks you're obliged to interact with, folks like, for instance, your editor, literary agent, or publicist.

Empathy is a word from developmental psychology. If our parents were genuinely responsive to our needs, it is likely that we developed an ability to empathize with others. But millions of people, perhaps even the vast majority, had a poorer experience that resulted in lifelong relational difficulties. However, even if they had that poorer experience in childhood, it is their job in adulthood to heal those wounds and make the conscious decision to treat the people around them decently.

Empathy is essentially the ability to understand another person's thoughts and feelings and the desire to do just that. It is both understanding *and* willingness. It is the mind-reading, feeling-reading ability built into each of us that many people have trouble accessing or do not much want to access. It is in many ways an inconvenient ability, because it makes the people around us real—and how much more convenient if they remain unreal!

Why is it important to empathize? It's important for all sorts of simple, straightforward reasons—but let's focus on its importance for the sake of your career as a creative person. If you don't really "get" what marketplace players are thinking and feeling you are much less likely to be able to deal with them or sell to them. The better you understand other people, the better are your chances for success.

Let's take a simple example. You sell a book to an editor. The book comes out. You present her with an idea for a second book and she declines. If you take her "no" at face value and don't take an interest in trying to fathom what she is thinking and feeling or what is going on in her world, all that you are left with is a 'no.' If instead you empathize with her as a person and with her in her position as editor, at the very least you've created the chance to get some more information. That information may make all the difference both with respect to selling her this second book and with selling *anyone* this second book.

Empathizing here means understanding your editor's reality. This has two separate and different meanings: understanding her as a person and understanding her role in her publishing house. Is she, as a *person*, someone who makes snap decisions but who can then be invited to rethink her snap decision based on rational arguments? Is she, as an *editor*, someone who has to answer to a lot of people about her decisions and who therefore needs to be armed—by you—with lots of good ammunition to present to those other people? If you don't know these things, then you won't know how much ammunition to present her with when you propose a project or how to help her change her mind after she's said "no" to a project.

In this particular usage of the word "empathy," its proper antonym is not "unfeelingness" but "misunderstanding." The proof that we are not empathizing with people is that we find ourselves not understanding where people are coming from. To take a simple example, if you send your editor an email and you somehow take it personally that she hasn't replied to you in twenty-four hours, you are almost surely misunderstanding where she is coming from in not answering quickly. Especially if you have given her something that she actually has to think about, it should follow that she needs some time to think about it!

Most creatives are susceptible to these misunderstandings for two primary reasons. The first is that they don't get sufficient opportunity to deal with marketplace players and as a result don't have a clear picture of who they are, how they operate, and what their universe looks like. The second is that because marketplace players matter so much to them and make them so anxious, they can't think very clearly about who these people really are. What can help? The following.

When you're obliged to deal with such a person, go to the room that is your mind, proceed directly to your well-stocked closet, and put on a pair of that person's shoes. Marketplace players are lionized, demonized, fantasized about, and so on—but rarely thought about clearly. By putting on such a person's shoes, you give yourself the opportunity to think as clearly about him or her as you possibly can!

Primary Issue: Insufficient Empathy

- What other issues might this exercise help address?
- How might you personalize and customize this exercise?
- What are five thoughts that would align with and support this exercise's central intention?
- What five actions might you take so as to support any changes you consider important to make?
- How might you use your imagination and your native brilliance to customize this exercise, upgrade your personality, improve your

experience of indwelling, or meet the challenge this exercise is addressing?

- Imagine that a quick, radical transformation in the direction suggested by this exercise might be possible. What might that transformation look like?

54 Day-Job Skin

Some smart, sensitive, creative individuals find themselves in careers or professions that allow them to both earn money and do their creative work. A given independent filmmaker makes just enough from his films that he doesn't also need a day job. A given astronomer has the academic job that allows him access to the huge telescope he requires. A given visual artist earns enough from her paintings to live well. A given writer works in a genre that actually earns her money.

Most creatives, however, must do work other than their creative work in order to pay the bills. They then face a double ignominy, that they must spend all those hours at this other work and that they find it hard, psychologically speaking, to leave their day job after their shift ends. At home after work, they are still brooding about some interaction at work, some criticism they received, some task they could have handled better, or some retort they might have delivered. What chance do they have to work on their novel if *this* is what they are thinking about?

Some years ago, I was visiting with an editor at a well-known magazine in her midtown Manhattan skyscraper offices. I commented on the chairs in the waiting room, which were shaped sort of like bar stools but which were pointy, tall, and sadistically uncomfortable. I said to her, "Wow, those chairs seem not only uncomfortable but uncomfortable on purpose." To which she replied, "That's our boss. He makes everything uncomfortable on purpose."

The day jobs that creatives must tolerate are not just time-eaters and energy-drainers but they are also theaters of the absurd where bosses have the power to pick out sadistic chairs for everyone to sit on—and do so. When you are battered by your day job in such ways, when what you are thinking about as you ride home to Queens on the subway is not your new painting but your revenge fantasies, how easy is it to get to your art?

How well do you leave your day job behind you at the end of the day? Are you still angry with your boss for something he said or did or have you left him at work? There is a famous Zen story that goes as follows. A master and an acolyte are walking home through the woods. They come to a stream.

A beautiful young woman is on the bank, unwilling to cross because she doesn't want to get her dress wet. The master offers to carry her across. She agrees. Later, as the master and the acolyte continue their walk home, the acolyte chides the master: "We aren't supposed to carry women like that!" The master laughs and replies, "I left that woman on the bank a long time ago. *You* are still carrying her!"

In order to create, we must leave at the studio door our grudges, our worried thoughts, our grievances, our revenge fantasies, and everything else from our day job that may be burdening our mind. If we continue to carry them, we may not make it to the studio at all. Are you spending more time brooding than painting? If your boss provides you with sadistic chairs and all manner of tyrannies, can you leave that behind you when you leave work each day? Make sure to engage in that useful cognitive work: leave those sadistic chairs at the office and clear your mind for your creative work!

What can help in this regard? Try the following. Directly after work, go to the room that is your mind. Head to that useful closet of yours, the one where you go to shed your heavy winter overcoat, your straitjacket, and your public persona costumes, the one where you keep all those shoes that you use to practice empathy, and remove your day job like a snake shedding its skin. Completely remove it. You do not want a vestige of your day job to remain.

Slide off that skin, stuff it in a box at the bottom of your closet, take a momentary mental shower to remove any sticky bits, and feel free. If you do not quite feel free yet, shower a bit longer. If you must brood a few seconds longer, get that brooding out of your system. Step out of that mental shower stall free of your day job. Then relax, if relaxing is the next right thing to do, hug your mate, if hugging your mate is the next right thing to do, or get to your creative work, if that is the next right thing to do. Whatever you decide is the next right thing for you to do, engage in it free of your day-job skin.

Primary Issue: Shedding Your Day Job

- What other issues might this exercise help address?
- How might you personalize and customize this exercise?
- What are five thoughts that would align with and support this exercise's central intention?
- What five actions might you take so as to support any changes you consider important to make?
- How might you use your imagination and your native brilliance to customize this exercise, upgrade your personality, improve your experience of indwelling, or meet the challenge this exercise is addressing?
- Imagine that a quick, radical transformation in the direction suggested by this exercise might be possible. What might that transformation look like?

55 Comparison-Free Zone

Say that you're a visual artist. You're likely to sometimes find yourself in one of the following situations:

- You enter a juried competition, one of your paintings is accepted for the competition, and, although you discover that you haven't won a coveted ribbon, you nevertheless attend the gala opening of the exhibition.
- You attend a large trade show where artist materials of every conceivable sort are displayed and where well-known artists give technique and materials demonstrations, some of which you attend.
- You spend a week at the annual or biennial convention of your medium (for example, the biennial International Association of Pastel Societies convention), where you take workshops and get to see the juried and award-winning work of well-known artists.

What are some of the psychological repercussions of attending events of this sort? Typically, there are both powerful positive emotions and powerful negative emotions generated by such attendance. Not so long ago I spent four days in Albuquerque at the pastel societies convention, where I was giving the keynote address. I talked with many artists—and here's what I heard. These artists were inspired to be among other pastel artists who had come from all over the world—China, Europe, Australia, New Zealand, Canada, etc.—and who constituted their tribe. Often isolated in their individual studios, they loved the camaraderie, the shared love of the medium of pastel, the excitement of learning about new products, and the sheer fun of the lively events organized throughout the convention.

At the same time, they couldn't keep themselves from doing a lot of comparing. The juried exhibition that was a featured part of the convention contained one beautiful work after another. It was hard for the less experienced artists and even for many of the pros not to hear themselves saying, "Wow, that's better than what I do." Many artists told me that they were leaving the convention with very mixed emotions: they felt inspired, on the one hand, and quite demoralized, on the other.

What can you do to deal with negative psychological consequences of this sort? For one thing, create a comparison-free zone in the room that is your mind. It might even be a whole second room with its own furnishings and fixtures. In this room, no comparisons are permitted. When you sit on the sofa in this room, you never hear yourself saying "Bob is doing so well" or "Mary has such great technique." You only hear yourself saying things like, "What does my work need from me today?" and "I can't wait to get to my work!"

Among my clients who have the hardest time of it are those who keep track of the successes of their peers. They know who's won which prize, whose new book has just been published to rave reviews, whose music video has crossed a hundred million views, whose solo show sold out. Often, they will claim to be simply keeping up with industry news, as if news of that sort had no negative psychological repercussions. It is almost as if they are testing themselves: let me see if I can tolerate hearing about the success of others without falling apart. They are about as successful at that as an alcoholic who tests himself by spending every night in a bar.

One client, a singer/songwriter, fixated on the touring schedule of a relatively well-known independent recording artist who regularly traveled worldwide. My client knew this artist's schedule virtually by heart—a London venue, followed by a Brighton venue, followed by a Manchester venue, followed by stops in Wales and Scotland, then off to Paris—and paid no attention to landing gigs of her own. Was it easier and safer to be envious of her putative rival than to put herself out into the world? Indeed, almost nothing is harder than letting go of fixations of this sort.

Keep comparisons to a minimum. To that end, create a dedicated space in the room that is your mind where no comparisons are permitted. It would be a shame if you had to stop attending industry events and missed out on visiting with your tribe just because the negative emotions that such events generated became too hard to handle. Likewise, it would be a shame if you used such comparing to sabotage yourself and keep yourself from succeeding. Instead, when you find yourself succumbing to comparisons or indulging in comparisons, hurry to that comparison-free zone in the room that is your mind and declare an end to comparing.

Primary Issue: Dealing with the Pain and Distress of Comparisons

- What other issues might this exercise help address?
- How might you personalize and customize this exercise?
- What are five thoughts that would align with and support this exercise's central intention?
- What five actions might you take so as to support any changes you consider important to make?

- How might you use your imagination and your native brilliance to customize this exercise, upgrade your personality, improve your experience of indwelling, or meet the challenge this exercise is addressing?
- Imagine that a quick, radical transformation in the direction suggested by this exercise might be possible. What might that transformation look like?

56 Ice Cube Tray

Creatives often resist doing their creative and intellectual work. Why? Because the work can be arduous. Because your current work, although not finished, may already disappoint you. Maybe it's proving deathly boring. Or maybe you have hard choices to make, about where to take the plot of your novel or how to follow up on the success of your first gallery show.

Maybe your to-do list of chores and responsibilities is making itself felt and demanding your attention. Maybe you're beginning to feel that your current project is very like something you did before. Even if nothing seems to be wrong or off, even if everything seems just fine, we can *still* feel resistant to sitting down and getting started. Often it seems as if there's a thin layer of ice between us and our creative work, a layer of resistance that we have to forcibly crack through, sometimes on a daily basis.

What can help? Well, cracking through that ice!

You know that crackling sound that a twistable ice cube tray makes when you twist it and loosen the ice cubes? That's a sound most of us know well. Let's make use of that knowledge. Stock the room that is your mind with a small refrigerator with a tiny freezer compartment, one just big enough to hold a single plastic tray of ice cubes. You can use the refrigerated section to keep the most expensive treats in the world, since you don't actually have to buy them, or you can store your homelier goodies there—maybe your daily cucumber and carrot snack—but reserve the freezer section for your resistance-busting ice cube tray.

How might you use your ice cube tray? You might ceremonially go the room that is your mind every day before your daily creative stint, open the refrigerator, remove the ice cube tray, and give it a mighty twist. What great crackling! Experience your resistance cracking as that ice cracks. Put the ice cube tray away—no need to refill it, as you haven't actually used any of the ice cubes you loosened—and hurry off to begin your creative work.

Or you might reserve this exercise for times when you feel particularly stuck and unmotivated. A day has passed without creating; two days have passed without creating; in the blink of eye, a month has vanished. You know that you had better do something—and now you know exactly what to do. Begin by warming yourself before the fire burning in your mind's eye fireplace, so as to rekindle your own motivational flame. Then crack some ice. Fire and ice! Isn't it likely that you'll immediately be able to get back to work?

Or you might try some alternate cracking exercise of your own creation, in case twisting an ice cube tray doesn't produce the result you want, that is, you blasting through your resistance. You might crack an egg against the side of a bowl. You might walk out on a lake on a bright winter's day and feel the ice cracking under your feet. You might smash a vase against the wall. You might crack a pitched ball with a baseball bat. In your mind's eye, you can try out anything. Create a variety of cracking exercises and give each one a try. Maybe you'll land on one that feels just right and that becomes your go-to resistance buster.

This cracking process can work for long-standing blocks, too. Many creatives suffer from the anxiety state called perfectionism. Their fear of imperfection causes them to refuse to create until they've acquired some internal guarantee that what they're about to create will prove excellent. But the realities of the creative process preclude such guarantees. As a result, they wait and wait and maybe never begin. Cracking something—an egg, a sheet of ice, a glass rendering of the word "perfect"—can help with this sort of long-standing block just as it can help with everyday resistance. It's certainly worth a try!

Creating just the right cracking experience will help you break through everyday resistance and dissolve longstanding blocks. Few things are as disappointing as not getting to your creative work. It may be exactly the thinnest veneer of ice that regularly stands between you and your work and all that is needed is a gentle tap—or a good rap—in order to crack through. Do that tapping or rapping, twist that ice cube tray and hear that wonderful crackling, and get on with your work.

Primary Issue: Resistance and Blockage

- What other issues might this exercise help address?
- How might you personalize and customize this exercise?
- What are five thoughts that would align with and support this exercise's central intention?
- What five actions might you take so as to support any changes you consider important to make?
- How might you use your imagination and your native brilliance to customize this exercise, upgrade your personality, improve your experience of indwelling, or meet the challenge this exercise is addressing?
- Imagine that a quick, radical transformation in the direction suggested by this exercise might be possible. What might that transformation look like?

57 Still-Life with Apricots

The creative process is harder to tolerate than most people, creatives included, imagine. It is hard to tolerate for all of the following reasons and for many more as well:

- Only a percentage of the work that we do turns out well, and only a percentage of that percentage is really excellent, meaning that we have many "failed" efforts to endure.
- The creative process involves making one choice after another (for instance, "Should I send my character here or should I send my character there?") and choosing provokes anxiety.
- The creative process involves going into the unknown, which can prove scary, especially if where we are going is into the recesses of our own psyche.
- The task we set ourselves—unraveling this scientific knot, creating this full-scale opera—may be beyond our intellectual or technical capabilities or may require information and understanding that we don't currently possess.
- The thing called "inspiration," which is one of the great joys of process and without which our work may prove lifeless, comes only periodically and can't be produced on demand.

A main headline as to why the creative process can feel so daunting is that not everything creatives attempt will turn out beautifully, that many efforts will turn out just ordinary, and that a significant number will prove flat-out not very good. A composer writes a hit Broadway musical—and the next one is abysmal. No one can believe it's the same person! A novelist pens a brilliant first novel—and the second one is unreadable. What a disappointment! A physicist comes *this close* to a breakthrough—but doesn't break through, rendering his several years of work "worthless." How demoralizing! These are everyday occurrences in the lives of creatives and the rule rather than the exception.

What to do? Of course, do everything required to make the work good, including getting quiet, showing up, honestly appraising, and all the rest. But in addition to all that, maturely accept the reality of missteps, mistakes, messes, lost weeks and even lost years, unhappy outcomes, and all the rest. To help with this effort at maturity, do the following. Hang a still-life painting of a bowl of apricots on a wall in the room that is your mind. Have that bowl be filled with gorgeous, ripe apricots and also with mottled, discolored overripe apricots. The lesson of this painting? You must calmly and gracefully take the bad with the good.

A romantic painter would make sure to paint only gorgeous apricots. Likewise, a super-realist painter in preparing his still life for copying would pick the best apricots to include, unless he was intending to make a point about decay. Virtually no painter, past or present, would fill his bowl with beautiful *and* rotten apricots. That goes against our ingrained ideas about beauty and about what a painting is "supposed to do." The painting you hang, however, is not being hung for its beauty. It is being hung there to remind you about the reality of process. It is being hung there to remind you that you must take the bad with the good as you create. It is being hung there to remind you to be your most mature self, the you who understands that you are bound to produce work all along the spectrum from lousy to brilliant.

Among his hundreds of cantatas, Bach's most famous cantata is number 140. His top ten would likely be comprised of numbers 4, 12, 51, 67, 80, 82, 131, 140, 143 and 170. What about the others? Are some merely workmanlike and unmemorable? Yes. Are some not very interesting at all? Yes? Was Bach obliged to live with that reality? Yes. As must you. You might produce a brilliant first thing and then never try again and so insure your success rate at 100 per cent. But is that a way to live a life? Or is that a way to avoid living?

Hang a painting of a bowl of apricots filled with lovely ripe apricots and unlovely overripe apricots in a prominent place on one of the walls in the room that is your mind. It is not there to reprimand you, chastise you, or discourage you. Rather, it is there to remind you about the reality of process, a reality that no human being can escape or evade. Every once in a while, maybe when your creative or intellectual work is going poorly or when you've created something that fails to meet your standards, stand in front of that painting, sigh, and murmur, "Process." Process is what is; honoring its reality and calmly living with that reality are choices you get to make.

Primary Issue: Enduring the Rigors and Realities of the Creative Process

- What other issues might this exercise help address?
- How might you personalize and customize this exercise?

- What are five thoughts that would align with and support this exercise's central intention?
- What five actions might you take so as to support any changes you consider important to make?
- How might you use your imagination and your native brilliance to customize this exercise, upgrade your personality, improve your experience of indwelling, or meet the challenge this exercise is addressing?
- Imagine that a quick, radical transformation in the direction suggested by this exercise might be possible. What might that transformation look like?

58 Pad of Checklists

Creatives often near the finish line on a creative project and then fail to complete it. Why does this happen so regularly? Here are four of many reasons, framed from the point of view of a painter:

- The painting-in-progress doesn't match the artist's original vision for the piece. Very often an artist "sees" her painting before it's painted—sees it in all its beauty, grandeur, and excellence—and then, as she paints, the "real" painting in front of her doesn't match the brilliance and perfection of her original vision. Disappointed, she loses motivation to complete her creative project and either white-knuckles her way to the end or in fact doesn't complete it.
- She fears that this is her best idea and that she may not have another excellent one ever. The brain can fool you into thinking that your current idea is the last excellent idea you'll ever have. You can get weighed down by the feeling that since no other idea will ever come to you, you had better nurse this one—so as to have something to work on and so as to put off what you feel will be a terrible moment of reckoning when, with this painting done, you'll face the void and discover that you have nothing available to say and nothing left to say.
- She fears losing her current good feelings. Say that you're currently doing a series of red paintings. All that red is making you feel buoyant and joyful. You have it in your mind that you will do a blue series next; and while that makes sense to you intellectually and aesthetically, it doesn't move your heart that much. These red paintings feel wonderful to you; the coming blue feels a little cool, verging on cold. So as to keep this loving feeling alive, you decide just out of conscious awareness not to finish these red paintings. You just want a little more time with them! So, you don't complete them.
- She's not feeling ready for the process to start all over again. Many artists find starting each new work of art something of a trial and even a little traumatic. At the moment of needing to begin they pester themselves with questions like, "Do I have another good idea in me?" or "Am I really working in the right style?" or "Will this be just another one of my paintings that no one

wants?" Because beginning is so painful a process for them, they prefer to keep working on their current project, even if it is done or could readily be completed, rather than face the unpleasant reality of another blank canvas.

- The appraising will then have to begin. While you're working on a piece, you can keep saying to yourself, "Yes, maybe it isn't wonderful yet, but by the end it will be!" You hold out the carrot that your further efforts will transform the work into something you really love. But once you say it is complete, then you actually have to appraise it and decide if it is or isn't excellent, or even any good because we want to put off that moment of reckoning, we are inclined to say, "Well, let me do just a little more." As a result, we continue to tinker, often ruining the work.

What can help with this problem of not completing enough of your work? The following. Keep a pad of "completion checklists" in a drawer in the room that is your mind. If you're building a house and you're approaching the end of the project, you create a punch list of last things that have to get done: spot painting, putting in a last light fixture, and so on. When you've completed everything on your punch list, you can be pretty certain that you are done. By contrast, a creative likely has no such checklist or punch list, would probably never dream of creating one, and, even if the concept popped into his head, would probably have no idea what to put on such a list.

A literal completion checklist for each of your projects might prove invaluable. But here I'm suggesting a metaphorical one. You need not actually list the tasks that remain before your work is done, you only need to pull out your pad of completion checklists, tear off the top one, and experience the sensation of intending to complete your current project. You are using your literal checklist, if you create one, to name your remaining tasks but you are using this checklist, the one that exists in the room that is your mind, to create a feeling. It is the feeling of "I intend to finish, and sooner rather than later!"

Primary Issue: Not Completing One's Creative Work

- What other issues might this exercise help address?
- How might you personalize and customize this exercise?
- What are five thoughts that would align with and support this exercise's central intention?
- What five actions might you take so as to support any changes you consider important to make?
- How might you use your imagination and your native brilliance to customize this exercise, upgrade your personality, improve your experience of indwelling, or meet the challenge this exercise is addressing?
- Imagine that a quick, radical transformation in the direction suggested by this exercise might be possible. What might that transformation look like?

59 Grandeur Corner

The room that is your mind can have as many nooks and corners as you like. You installed a speaker's corner in a previous exercise. In this chapter, I'd like you create a grandeur corner that you visit to remind you that grandeur is valuable and that grandeur is available.

We tend to associate the word "grandeur" with events like royal weddings and sights like the Grand Canyon. Hotels are grand, canals are grand, and cruise ships are grand. But something about that way of thinking prevents us from demanding grandeur from the other stuff of existence, like an image that we craft, a jam that we jar, or a kiss that we give. For more reasons than we can count, grandeur isn't very present in our daily lives.

In all the meetings that I've ever attended—faculty meetings, business meetings, meetings of therapists, and meetings of artists—I've never heard anyone say, "What's wanted is a little more grandeur." Have you? On the long list of things discussed when people gather, grandeur never appears. There are no parties honoring it, no organizations devoted to it, no lobbyists buttonholing members of Congress and whispering, "Support the grandeur bill and we'll make it worth your while!"

I remember sitting in a sterile coffee-break room in a suite of offices, writing by hand before the class I taught began. In a corner of the room were some boxes of computer parts. There was a soda machine, a microwave, a copy machine, a fire extinguisher, a sink, a wastepaper basket, and a metal cabinet for office supplies. The walls were a dull blue-gray, the round table at which I sat was the same dull blue-gray, and so were the chairs and the floor.

But on the wall across from me was a poster of a Manuel Neri oil-on-paper called *Alberica No. 1*. It portrayed a woman with a blue face, a yellow torso, and burgundy legs. The top half of the background was a brilliant yellow and the bottom half was a striking blue. If I hadn't had it or something like it on the wall to look at, I would surely have died of grandeur deprivation in a room like that.

Think about your own life. What last stirred feelings of grandeur in you? Was it something you saw on the commute to your day job, some reality show episode, or something you experienced at a meeting? Probably not. My hunch is that you were last stirred by music, a film, a passage in a book or a piece of art. You stopped, listened to the music, and said to yourself "How beautiful!" or "How powerful!" or "This is good stuff!" You were transported. In the back of your mind you whispered "I should be creating and doing work this strong." You said to yourself, but maybe not in such a way that you could hear the message clearly, "Without this beauty I would die."

The painter Max Beckmann once said, "All important things in art have always originated from the deepest feeling about the mystery of Being." I think that this sentiment comes close to capturing the origins of our sense of grandeur. We are built to appreciate mystery, to harbor deep feelings, to contemplate the universe with its marvelous quirks and distinguishing features. To bring less than all of this to the art-making experience is to bring only a shadow of our inheritance. Without a Neri on the wall, Mozart in the air or Tolstoy in our hands we would wither away, no matter how good the benefits and stock options at our day job. We need grandeur to survive.

You can remind yourself of this necessity by installing a grandeur corner in the room that is your mind. Here you hold the intention to create something powerful, beautiful, admirable, meaningful, resonant, and grand. Here you remind yourself that grandeur is available and that you can create it yourself. What is actually in this corner? That's for you to decide. Maybe it's filled with music. Maybe on a chalkboard is the scientific formula that always stirs you. Maybe you'll repeat some of the items from your altar, choosing those that most evoke the feelings of awe, grandeur, and mystery.

Nothing in your grandeur corner may look grand in any traditional sense. I'd be surprised if you installed marble staircases and velvet drapes. You might even find very homey objects there: a stone from a river bed, a whimsical doll, a door somehow made grand by its layers of peeling paint. Create your grandeur corner now. Visit the room that is your mind, look around, pick a suitable nook or corner, and fill it in such a way that what you experience as you face it is grandeur. Then pack up that feeling and move directly to your creative work.

Primary Issue: Lack of Grandeur

- What other issues might this exercise help address?
- How might you personalize and customize this exercise?
- What are five thoughts that would align with and support this exercise's central intention?
- What five actions might you take so as to support any changes you consider important to make?

- How might you use your imagination and your native brilliance to customize this exercise, upgrade your personality, improve your experience of indwelling, or meet the challenge this exercise is addressing?
- Imagine that a quick, radical transformation in the direction suggested by this exercise might be possible. What might that transformation look like?

60 Mattering Sweater

It would seem self-evident that a smart, sensitive, creative person would decide to opt to matter and consider her efforts, if not dramatically important, at least not pointless. Why wouldn't she opt to matter and conceptualize her efforts as valuable?

Well, certainly, her upbringing might be one impediment. She might have grown up lectured about the extent to which she didn't matter and punished for attempting to matter. Her culture, too, may have drilled into her the idea that she was merely one of many and that group norms always come first: that religion comes first, fitting in comes first, not making waves comes first. Many life lessons might have taught her that it was wrong or pointless to opt to matter.

Still, the magnitude of her difficulty in opting to matter is not really explained even by these many negative life lessons. It turns out that the main obstacle she faces is her belief, shared by every modern person, that human life is "ultimately" meaningless. Any reasons that she tries to adduce for mattering are overwhelmed by the possibility, bordering on a certainty, that she and her fellow human beings are only excited matter put on earth for no reason except that the universe could do it. All life, hers included, is mere pointless happenstance, not worth crying about or taking seriously.

This bitter pill is a new view, barely two hundred years old. Before that, life seemed special. For thousands of years the idea of life as categorically different from non-life, unique and important in the cosmos, was a core tenet of philosophy. This view felt compelling until biologists found, beginning with Wohler and the synthesis of urea in 1828, that organic compounds could be created from inorganic materials. We can date our present difficulties in making and maintaining meaning from that single event, the synthesis of urea.

From that day forward a new philosophy was needed, since life lost much of its mystery, sanctity, importance, and glamour. Once you join the scientific materialists, as all of us have to a lesser or a greater degree, and believe that you can make human beings simply by striking dead atoms with powerful but meaningless forces, life turns meaningless. This is the basic problem with which we've been wrestling for two hundred years. The suspicion that we do not matter haunts and plagues those of us who are existential, even including believers.

We manage to bear up despite the suspicion that we are merely excited matter. We find ways to bear up every day. But on many days, we discover that we can't bear up; on those days, we despair about our cosmic unimportance and grow furious with the facts of existence. We feel saddened and defeated and lose our motivation to make meaning in any way. The very word "meaning" strikes our ears as a cosmic joke. Because of our fear that we are merely excited matter and the consequent grudge that we hold against the universe, we feel lost and alienated, like a refugee far from home in a universe that cares nothing for us.

What can help? A comfy sweater bearing the motto "I matter" or "My efforts matters" or some phrase that communicates to you the idea that you must opt to matter despite all your doubts about the universe. You put this imagined sweater on each time you enter the room that is your mind, perhaps at the same time that you remove your winter overcoat and your public persona costume. Inside that room, you live in that sweater. With that sweater on, you remember to matter.

Every modern person is driven to throw up her hands and cry, "Why bother! Why wrestle this stupid novel into existence? I might as well eat chocolate, take a bubble bath, and to hell with the ideas of life purpose choosing and meaning making!" So, she eats chocolate and takes a bubble bath. But within minutes she is forcibly struck by the counter-thought that meaning must have meaning, so devoid of meaning does it feel to have thrown up her hands. A countervailing energy arises in her, something like hope and something like pride, an energy that readies her to do combat with her sincere belief that she is utterly unimportant. Wearing her mattering sweater is one way to defeat meaninglessness.

We must opt for life. We must opt to live the twenty years or the sixty years ahead of us. This may be all that we have, but it is exactly what we have. We force life to mean while we are alive and until death releases us from our responsibility to live authentically. We say, "While I am alive, I can love." We say, "While I am alive, I can learn a few things." We say, "While I am alive, I can help in some ways." We say, "While I am alive, I can create." We opt to matter because we can and because, unromantically but utterly sincerely, we must.

Put on your mattering sweater. Rarely take it off.

Primary Issue: Combatting Meaninglessness

- What other issues might this exercise help address?
- How might you personalize and customize this exercise?

- What are five thoughts that would align with and support this exercise's central intention?
- What five actions might you take so as to support any changes you consider important to make?
- How might you use your imagination and your native brilliance to customize this exercise, upgrade your personality, improve your experience of indwelling, or meet the challenge this exercise is addressing?
- Imagine that a quick, radical transformation in the direction suggested by this exercise might be possible. What might that transformation look like?

In Conclusion

Human beings possess an inner life. This inner life ought to be the primary subject of psychology and the main concern of helpers and yet it isn't. This is truly odd and can't be explained by the fact that, since we can't see this inner life, we can't do a decent job of thinking about it or chatting about it. That can't be the reason for this amazing omission.

In psychology, we chat about unseen things all the time. We chat about things we call archetypes, the unconscious, the id, the ego, trauma-induced memories, distorted cognitions, homoerotic feelings, group identifications, and on and on. Why, then, have we taken a pass on chatting about that most salient and important of human experiences, each individual's inner life?

The answer to that question is beyond me. But the problem remains. If we do not seriously consider the therapeutic importance of dynamic self-regulation and the profound differences between healthy and unhealthy indwelling, we've tied our hands behind our backs as helpers and, as one consequence, are that much more likely to buy into the "mental disorder" paradigm. To the extent that we ignore a person's inner life, to exactly that extent will we be inclined to claim that, when he announces that he is suffering, we'll respond with a false, pseudo-medical diagnosis.

The sixty exercises in this book serve two primary purposes: they make you, as a helper, more aware of the reality that each of us indwells, and they can improve the quality of that indwelling for anyone who actually engages with the exercises. If a client's inner life is currently experienced as torturous and, as a result of entertaining these exercises, it becomes calmer, airier, and altogether more self-friendly, that client has really been helped. That change amounts to healing and transformation.

How we live in the room that is our mind, the stories that we tell ourselves there, the pressures that we experience there, the slights that we magnify there, the grievances that we stew about there, the unfulfilled dreams that we pine about there, the very look of that place—how drab it is, how airless it is, how stifling it is—is the equivalent of our mental health. To me, it is a kind of absurdity to talk about a person's mental health and not talk about her inner reality.

I hope you agree. Whether you embrace my metaphor of "the room that is your mind" as a good way of speaking about that inner reality or whether you prefer some other metaphor, I hope you agree that the key to helping is aiding a person in arriving at a more aware, self-regulated, self-friendly, and pain-free inner reality. These exercises can help in that regard. If you are a helper, I hope that you will offer them to your clients. If you are a sufferer, I hope that you will give them a try.

Index

Made in the USA
Middletown, DE
12 July 2019